'TIL THE BOYS COME HOME

'TIL THE BOYS COME HOME

Great Rissington soldiers

Clare Mayo

Reveille
PRESS

Reveille Press is an imprint of
Tommies Guides Military Booksellers & Publishers

Gemini House
136-140 Old Shoreham Road
Brighton
BN3 7BD

www.tommiesguides.co.uk

First published in Great Britain by
Reveille Press 2013

For more information please visit
www.reveillepress.com

© 2013 Clare Mayo

A catalogue record for this book is available
from the British Library

All rights reserved. Apart from any use under UK copyright law no part of this publication may be reproduced, stored in a retreival system, or transmitted, in any form or by any means, without prior written permission of the publisher, nor be otherwise circulated in any form of binding or cover other than that in which it is published and without a similar condition being imposed on the subsequent publisher.

ISBN 978-1-908336-47-7

Cover design by Reveille Press

Printed and bound in Great Britain by
CPI Antony Rowe, Chippenham and Eastbourne

Contents

Acknowledgements 9
Foreword 11
Preface. 13
To war and back 15

Part One – To war and back
The Village. 17
Enlistment. 19
Training And Equipment. 23
The Frontline 27
Demobilisation 31
Remembrance 33

Part Two – The soldiers 35
Mervyn Berry 37
Frank Bartlett 47
The Bolter Boys 51
   Fred Bolter 53
   Will Bolter 57
Joe Cambray 63
Arthur Cyphus. 69
Arnold Hathaway 73
Wilfrid Hensley 77
Albert Higgins 89
Fred Howse 93
Tom Hyatt 99
Harry Lane 103
Lol Lane 107
Percy Lewis 111
Cecil Mace. 113

Fred Masters	119
The Mills Boys	125
Frank Mills	127
William Mills	131
Garnet Morris	135
Teddy Parker	141
The Pill Boys	143
Will Pill	145
Harry Pill	149
Bert Pill	151
Oliver Porter	153
Charles Pratley	161
The Pratley Boys	167
Jack Pratley	169
Bob Pratley	177
George Rachael	183
Percy Smith	189
The Souls Boys	193
Bert Souls	195
Fred Souls	199
Walter Souls	205
Alf Souls	209
Arthur Souls	213
Tom Spencer	217
The Vellender Boys	221
Fred Vellender	223
Jack Vellender	227
Charlie White	231
Part Three – The Battlefields Today	235
Abbreviations and terms used in war diaries	243
Resources	245

*To my darling father
Len Berry
The best of men*

Acknowledgements

Some information on individual men, has been given verbally from family members, for which I am especially grateful. My thanks go to:

Leonard and Leslie Berry, Arthur Lane, Mabel Herbert, Phil Pratley, Marjorie Hicks, Deanna Bullwinkle, John Rachael, Joyce Coles, Tina Lester, Tony Peachey, Steve Eeles, Jean Greenhill, Elsie Sollis, Stephen Hook and Maud Pill, whose Fathers, Grandfathers and Uncles are featured on these pages and who contributed their time and material.

Also a special thanks to:

Jeremy Banning and Matt Leonard for all their encouragement and support,
and The Reverend Sue Moth, St John the Baptist Church
Members of the 1914-1918 forum
Cheltenham Library
David Read, Soldiers of Gloucestershire Museum
Amanda Goode, College Archivist, Cambridge University
Berkshire Records Office
Andrew Finch, Berkshire Yeomanry Museum
The Machine Gun Corps Old Comrades Association
Hugh Babington Smith, Soldiers of Oxfordshire Trust
Anne Furze, Lillington Parish Church

Foreword

ALTHOUGH I VISIT the Cotswolds from time to time I have never been to Great Rissington. Yet, despite this omission I still find a connection with the village. When Clare Mayo and I were discussing the casualties listed on the village's war memorial she talked of the famous Souls brothers; five local boys who answered their country's call and never returned. As a parent the loss of any child would be unimaginable but to lose five boys to the war is beyond our comprehension. Years before I had been on a battlefield trip where one of our party, Stan, an ex-Guardsmen, had suggested stopping at Bully-Grenay Communal Cemetery in the drab, flat coalfields of Artois. Stan had read about the Souls brothers in the Daily Mirror and requested a stop to pay his respects at the grave of one of the boys. Gathered around the headstone we listened as Stan recounted the family's loss, how Albert had been the first of the brothers to enlist and the first to die. Despite many personal visits made to soldiers graves over subsequent years I have always remembered that visit and the heart-rending story of the 'Souls brothers'. And now I am here with the chance to write the foreword to a book honouring them and all men of Great Rissington. Coincidence or fate?

Today's visitors to the battlefields are often overwhelmed at the scale of loss. British fatalities from the ongoing conflict in Afghanistan are reported widely on the news – and quite rightly so – but those losses are incomparable to that suffered by the British Expeditionary Force from 1914-18. Day-to-day casualties sustained in simply holding the line were known by the distasteful term 'natural wastage'; thousands of men killed or wounded every week without any grand advance. Set-piece battles swelled the casualty lists further with alarming ease. With our twenty-first century sensibilities we become anaesthetised to these numbers; five hundred casualties sustained here, a thousand there. It is only when we focus on the individual and form a personal connection that the true cost of warfare becomes apparent. That simple connection reinforces the importance of studies such as this.

This book covers essential information on the village, men's enlistment, training and posting overseas plus a précis of frontline conditions as well as a look at the demobilisation process and post-war remembrance. The vast majority of the book, however, concentrates on the men's individual stories. Biographical information is provided along with a summary of the situation in each sector. The use of battalion war diaries and personal letters completes the picture. Most importantly, it is not only the dead whose story is told but also the forgotten majority; the men who served and came back to pick up the pieces of their pre-war life. Clare Mayo's perseverance and dedication to this project is commendable, clearly evidenced in her quest to visit the graves and memorials where Great Rissington men are commemorated. For filling a gap in the history of the village she deserves our thanks.

Jeremy Banning
Bristol, September 2012

Preface

I FIRST BECAME INTERESTED in First World War soldiers from Great Rissington after tracing my family tree and looking into my own Grandfather's war service. He had said very little about his time in the army to his sons. Like most of the men who had served, he just didn't want to talk about it. He was a private in the Machine Gun Corps and that was about all anyone knew. It was whilst I was in the Public Record Office at Kew, looking for his Service Records, that I thought it would be interesting to find out about all the other men from Great Rissington who had fought in the First World War.

It has taken several years to research the individual stories and I hope I have done them justice. I have had a lot of help and support from my husband and from family members of the soldiers, without whom I would never have been able to discover names and details. Nearly 80% of the First World War Service Records were destroyed during the Blitz in the Second World War, and many of those that survived are burnt or water damaged. Officers' papers were kept in a separate place and are intact, which was helpful in the case of Wilfrid Hensley, whose family I was unable to trace. Many of the men were related by marriage and their descendants still live locally. Some family names died out because the only sons who carried the name were killed.

I have personally visited every man's grave or commemoration monument in France and Belgium. All the cemeteries on the Somme and in Belgium are beautifully kept, with English garden flowers growing on each grave. ('So that an English rose's shadow falls across every man's grave.') I was unable to visit the Doiran

Memorial in Greece, where Fred Vellender is commemorated, but a friend took photos for me and placed a poppy cross for him.

It has not been possible to trace living family members of some of the men, but by using the Battalion War Diaries, I have managed to show some of the actions they were involved in. Sadly, for some men, with no records to go on, this means their stories are very thin.

The battlefields in France and Belgium are long gone, but the traces of the war can still be seen by visitors today, including old trench lines and craters. The countryside on the Somme in particular, is very open and it is easy to see why the fighting here was so difficult. On a rainy day, the ground soon turns into a sticky mud which clings to your boots and everything else. Battlefield debris is still ploughed up by farmers today and the fields are full of chunks of shrapnel and old munitions.

I would like to thank my husband, Kevin, for all his hard work trawling through records at Kew and for assisting me in hunting down cemeteries in France and Belgium. I have enjoyed this project very much and hope my small contribution to these brave men's stories will ensure that their names are remembered with pride for the sacrifice and dedication to duty they gave.

Clare Mayo

Part One

To war and back

The Village

GREAT RISSINGTON IS a small North Cotswold village situated on the side of a hill, overlooking the Windrush Valley. The houses are built in the traditional style from the local Cotswold stone.

Great Rissington c1910 with 'Waterbank' on the right. The house attached was demolished in 1922.

The village, in 1914, was very much self-supporting, with five farms offering the main source of employment. In the 1911 census other occupations recorded are, Butcher, Haybinder, Mason, Mole Catcher, Wheelwright, Baker, House Decorator, Dressmaker, Blacksmith, Haytrusser and Carpenter.

When the call to arms came, there was no shortage of volunteers from the Parish and surrounding villages. Men from all walks of life joined up and went off to fight for their King and Country.

In 1917, my great, great Aunt Annie, (Edith A Smith), who had trained as a teacher at Great Rissington Board School and later became an author, wrote a poem for the men who were far from home. It was published in the Cheltenham and Gloucestershire Chronicle in the New Year.

> *We sing to-day of a year that's gone,*
> *Enveloped in border of mourning,*
> *Of many brave hearts that formed the throng,*
> *With honour the homeland crowning;*
> *Of those who died on the field of strife,*
> *Shedding their manhood's glory,*
> *Perchance uncrowned by the laurels' might,*
> *Deep set in our hearts the story.*
> *Patiently bearing the battle's fray,*
> *Mid din of the cannons roar,*
> *Losing their lives 'mong clouds of grey,*
> *Struggle in vain, nor gain the shore,*
> *Their names, un-named in the rush to-day,*
> *Will shine in the vista of years,*
> *Liberty, Freedom and Right will say,*
> *We rise out of thee, our cradle thy tears.*

A New Year, yet it was to be almost two more years until the war would be over. Life in the village went on as usual. The boys, fighting in France, Belgium and further afield may well have seen Annie's poem. Families sent local papers to the men in the trenches along with their letters and parcels. When the poem was published, six village boys had already laid down their lives for King and Country.

Enlistment

IN 1914, THE British Army consisted of professional regular soldiers, part-time members of the Territorial Force and soldiers of the Special Reserve. Joining the regulars, a man had to pass physical tests and enlist for a set period. The recruits had to be over 5 feet 3 inches, and aged between 19 and 38. When a man's service had ended, he then became a member of the Reserves.

The Territorial Force (TF) was formed in 1908 and gave men an opportunity to join the army on a part-time basis. Men trained in the evenings and at weekends, and spent time at a summer camp, very much like the modern Territorial Army today. The TF were very much a home defence unit and it was not mandatory to serve overseas.

If war broke out, it meant an immediate return to the colours for all men in the Reserve, which numbered 350,000 in 1914. On the day war was declared, 4 August 1914, General Mobilisation Notices were sent out to all reservists and the following day Field Marshal Earl Kitchener issued orders to increase the army. Both Britain and Germany believed the war would be over by Christmas but Kitchener thought otherwise. He decided to expand the regular army by raising a new body of men created from wartime volunteers. Men would sign up for a term of three years or for the duration of the war and serve overseas. On 6 August, Parliament agreed the number of men to be raised would be 500,000. A feeling of euphoria broke out and men from all walks of life responded to Kitchener's 'Call to Arms', when he asked for 100,000 men to volunteer aged between 19 and 30. Adverts began to appear in the local papers to encourage volunteers.

Advertisements in the Evesham Journal 1914

Recruiting Sergeants held rallies where speeches were made and a band often played rousing tunes. Men would fall in behind the band and march to the recruiting office, swept along with the excitement. Once there, they would fill in their forms known as attestation and take 'the Kings Shilling'. Most people believed that the allies would be victorious.

A batch of Bourton and district recruits off to serve their King and Country (Cheltenham Chronicle 1914)

ENLISTMENT

By 21 August the first 100,000 men had come forward. These men formed the New Army or K1 and were known as Kitchener's Men.

Men from Great Rissington and the surrounding Parishes were enlisted at Bourton on the Water and Stow on the Wold. At the start of the war, men could often have a choice of Regiment, and could attend a depot or recruiting office for a particular unit. Later on men were encouraged to join Regiments that needed new recruits to strengthen their numbers.

Recruits for the 11th Glosters at Stow on the Wold, August 1915
(The Cheltenham Chronicle and Gloucestershire Graphic)

After attesting, the new recruits went home and awaited their joining instructions. Britain, unlike France and Germany, had no conscription. In early 1915, the Government realised that voluntary recruitment was not going to raise the numbers of men needed. Almost two in every five men were unfit for the army. The National Registration Act was passed on 15 July 1915, as a step towards reviving recruitment. Men who had been considered unfit previously could now be passed fit for active duty. There were a few men in Great Rissington who having failed the first time, now tried again and succeeded in joining up. The Government also use a rigorous poster campaign to encourage men to join up.

Gloucestershire Echo Saturday 15 May 1915
RECRUITING ON THE COTSWOLDS
Messrs. T. Spink and R. W. Birkett of the Imperial Maritime League accompanied by Sergt. Smart of the Gloucesters, visited Bourton on the Water on Tuesday evening and held an open air recruiting meeting near the Victoria Hall. The speeches were illustrated by a series of lantern slides and at the close of the meeting six young men came forward and offered to join the Army. Four of these have been passed by the doctor.

Messrs. Spink and Birkett also held a meeting in the Square, Stow on the Wold on Wednesday evening, when Sergt. Terrell (of the Gloucesters) and Corpl. Holland (late of the Grenadier Guards) also spoke. Sergt. Smart was also in attendance. Six recruits were obtained. Despite the inclement weather there was a large attendance and the speaker's remarks were attentively listened to.

On 11 October 1915, Lord Derby introduced a system known as the Derby Scheme, for raising the numbers of volunteers. Men aged 18 to 41 could continue to enlist voluntarily, or attest with a duty to come if called up. It was also agreed that single men would be called up before married men. The men who attested under the Derby Scheme went home to await their call-up. Although a man had to be 18 to enlist, many boys added a few years to their age, and not too many questions were asked by the recruiting sergeants.

Eventually, the Government introduced the National Military Service Act in January 1916, which was basically conscription and all unmarried men aged 18 - 41 were enlisted. This also included married men by May 1916. Those men who thought they didn't qualify on grounds of occupation, health or conscientious objection could appeal to a local tribunal for an exemption certificate.

Training And Equipment

IN SMALL VILLAGES, like Great Rissington, men would parade on sports fields and practice drill, before moving to their base depot. The cricket ground, at Bourton on the Water, was used to drill local men who had enlisted. Training consisted of drill, marching, essential field craft etc. Later a soldier trained in his specialist field, such as machine gunner, rifleman, signaller and so on.

Drilling on Bourton Cricket grounds
(The Butt Studios, Bourton on the Water)

Before specially built camps were provided, with their own hospitals, canteens and other amenities, training facilities were established in large public buildings, such as, schools and halls. Initially, the army could not cope with such a massive increase in manpower and it took some time to make appropriate arrangements.

When an officer was granted a commission he was given an allowance to get fitted out with his kit. He would have his uniform made to measure at a gentleman's outfitters that specialised in regulation equipment. Below is a notice for Slade's, who advertised their services in the Cheltenham Chronicle in 1914.

For the ordinary rank and file, kit was issued from the Quartermaster's Stores as and when it was needed. With the initial rush to join up, there was a shortage of equipment and many men spent their first few weeks training in their 'civvies' and drilling with wooden rifles or brooms. Some battalions were issued with old blue uniforms until the shortages were sorted out. Many battalions, which were raised locally, had their uniforms provided by raising the funds themselves. When the men were eventually kitted out they would receive the following:

TRAINING AND EQUIPMENT

Tunic, Trousers, two shirts, boots, puttees, two pairs drawers, two pairs socks, vest, service cap with badge, greatcoat, webbing belt and pouches, pay book, cut-throat razor, toothbrush, towel, water bottles, knife, fork and spoon, rifle, bayonet and scabbard, mess tin and a haversack. Two ID discs were also issued, showing name, number, regiment and religion. If a man was killed, one disc was buried with him and the other sent to records.

*Digging trenches at a training camp, Cheltenham
(The Cheltenham Chronicle and Gloucestershire Graphic)*

Once fully trained, soldiers embarked on ships at Folkestone or Southampton for Le Havre or Boulogne, France. The training and drill continued in French base camps until the men were sent into the lines. Facilities for training were established in the rear areas, well away from the front. Some were huge camps of huts housing thousands of men, either on their way from basic training in England to a unit, or in the process of returning from hospital. One was the notorious Bull Ring at Etaples, which often housed 100,000 recruits at a time. The men were prepared for the trenches and had lectures on subjects such as lice, gas and trench foot.

Basic training taught a man personal and group discipline, such as following commands, saluting, marching and weapons drill. As a soldier was approaching duty on an active front, he would receive basic training in first aid, gas defence, wiring, etc. This training would still continue during active service. When the men went into the frontline trenches they also carried picks, entrenching tools, wire-cutters, bombs, 150 rounds of ammunition, a blanket, a waterproof sheet, and iron rations, which consisted of a tin of bully beef, tea, sugar and biscuits. This was all carried on or in a pack that could weigh up to 60lbs.

The Frontline

BRITISH SOLDIERS WERE known as 'Tommy Atkins' or 'Tommies' for short, and a typical Tommy was actually only at the front for about a quarter of his total time abroad. A large proportion of men never went into the frontlines at all. The frontlines were, of course, better known as the trenches. But behind these were the support trenches and supply lines, training camps, headquarters and stores.

Frontline trenches were usually about seven feet deep, six feet wide with a fire-step cut into the side. The front and rear of the trenches were known as the parapet and the parados. Trenches were generally not dug in a straight line to prevent the enemy from entering and firing along the line. They were also dug in sections, or bays, so that shell bursts were more contained. Duckboards were used to line the bottom to help keep trench foot under control. The men also made dugouts or funk holes in the sides to protect them from the weather.

The trenches were usually protected by belts of barbed wire in front and machine gun posts. Saps or short trenches were dug out from the trenches into no man's land as listening posts. The support and reserve trenches were behind the frontlines with communication trenches cut at an angle between all three.

Generally, men spent four days in the frontline, four days in reserve and four days at a rest camp. This wasn't always the case and many men would spend longer periods in the frontline owing to shortage of relief troops, inclement weather, battle conditions etc. Trench life was boring and hard work, as well as extremely dangerous. At dawn and dusk, the frontline troops were ordered to

'Stand To!' This meant standing on the fire step with fixed bayonet ready for any enemy attack. Dawn and dusk were the most popular time for enemy trench raids, owing to the poor light. Stand To came to be known as 'Morning Hate', for obvious reasons. At night, one man in four was posted as a sentry on lookout duty. Other men would repair trenches or go out into no man's land to put out wire, or perhaps take part in a trench raid on the enemy.

It was common for soldiers to name trenches after places they knew at home, such as Piccadilly Circus and Worcester Street, or to change the French place names into English sounding ones. Auchonvillers, on the Somme, was known as Ocean Villas to the Tommies and Mouquet Farm as Moo Cow or Mucky Farm.

In early 1915, there was little action in the frontlines and it was very much a case of 'live and let live' for both sides. During 1915 a letter was published in the Gloucestershire Echo from Gunner Wood of the machine gun section of the 1/5th Gloucestershire Regiment. He wrote about life in the trenches, referring to his position as 'Breezy Villa', somewhere in France.

Company Sergeant-Major William Bizley taking aim. 1/4th Battalion, The Gloucestershire Regiment. c. 1915.
Courtesy of The Soldiers of Gloucestershire Museum

> "Writing materials are scarce out here, but at the present moment time is plentiful, and I will try and give you some of the idea of home and mode of life. This is our second day in the trenches. Half a dozen of us form the team. I inhabit a little

dug-out or 'booby hatch' at the rear of the trench. You can't stand up in it and you can't lie the full length of it. It would not compare with the meanest Eskimo hut or Indian wigwam, but to us it is home and we love it. Four feet in height, it is about five feet square, three sides being composed of sandbags, and the fourth left open to form a door. A waterproof drops over this at night and with straw, waterproof and blanket, we sleep sound as tops and have to be almost dragged out for 'stand-to' at four in the morning. The roof – well the holes in the roof – act as ventilators and do not let in too much rain.

So much for our home, and in it we spend most of our time for there is little to do in the trenches. Of course there are the periodical turns of sentry to be done, when everyone turns out and stands for an hour behind the parapet. As to the rest of one's time, it is taken up with eating, sleeping and thinking of home. Ah! It is an exciting life this, but one that makes a man think highly of his home.

A little excitement comes at night when it is one's turn to fetch the rations from headquarters. Then the rule is, whenever a flare goes up, lie down flat on the ground, never mind the dirt. Ours is an advanced trench and consequently we have Germans in front of us, Germans to the right of us and Germans to the left of us.

These trenches have been occupied since October and the farmhouses around and a village near are absolutely in ruins. The enemy's guns are doing some firing now and every now and then a shell shrieks through the air above us and bursts with a great bang somewhere in the distance. The food we are getting is plentiful and good, but I have had neither a wash nor a shave since we came into the trenches and do not look like getting one until we go out.

We get fine rations – bacon, a loaf a day, jam, tea and sugar, potatoes, cheese and a tinned dinner which consists of meat and vegetables ready cooked."

Gunner Wood's letter gives a flavour of a soldier's life in the trenches. However, death was always present for those on frontline duties. Either by a direct shellfire hit, or sniper's bullet. Gunner Wood omits these details to reassure those left at home that he is not in any danger. One third of Allied casualties were sustained in the trenches.

Demobilisation

THE ARMISTICE WAS declared on 11 November 1918 and signed at 5am. It came into effect six hours later at 11am and was signed in Marshall Foch's railway carriage. Terms required Germany to leave all occupied territories within two weeks. Germany was in no fit state to continue the war and so accepted the conditions. The Versailles Peace Treaty, which followed was signed in 1919. The casualties for both sides were horrendous. Over eight million men had been killed or died, 21 million wounded and nearly eight million were prisoners or missing.

With the Armistice signed, there were celebrations all over Britain, with people dancing in the streets and having parties. Men began to think of home and their loved ones. Many men could not stand the silence after years of gunfire, and broke down. It would be a while before the Great Rissington soldiers returned to their village. Battlefields had to be cleared, munitions made safe and there were many other duties to perform before being demobbed.

For most men, early 1919 would be their homecoming time. They would slip back into their old lives and the majority of them would reveal little about their war experiences. Some old friends would never be returning and some lives would be changed forever. Often men moved away from the village to work in places such as Birmingham and further afield where the wages were better.

Photo by Butt Studios, Bourton on the Water.
Back row (Teddy Parker), Bob Pratley, Arthur Cyphus, Bert Pill, Will Pill, Unnamed
Middle Row Unnamed, Joe Cambray, Tom Hyatt, Frank Mills, Charlie White, Percy Lewis, Harry Lane
Front Row Albert Higgins, Fred Bolter, William Mills, Will Bolter, Charles Pratley, Fred Howse

Remembrance

AFTER THE WAR villages began to erect memorials in honour of those who had died. People wanted to remember the sacrifices made by their loved ones, friends and neighbours. Many people could not afford to visit the many cemeteries in France, Belgium and further afield. Massive monuments were also constructed on the battlefields to commemorate the thousands of men with no known grave. These include the Thiepval Memorial on the Somme, France and the Menin Gate in Ypres, Belgium.

*The carved memorial plaque inside St John the Baptist church
(N.B. Garnet Morris actually died in 1917)*

Great Rissington is unusual in that its war memorial, dedicated in 1922, is situated inside the village church. There is also a photographic display of the fallen which is a most poignant reminder of the tragic loss of life. There were 13 Great Rissington soldiers who would not return home and they are not forgotten.

The photographic display in the Church

Celebrating the coronation of George VI in 1937 with the men proudly wearing their war medals

Part Two

The soldiers

PART TWO OF this book consists of individual chapters about each soldier's war service. Some chapters will be more detailed than others, which is a reflection on the material I was able to discover and the relatives I was able to contact. Some soldier's stories will not be told in this book because despite several years of research I was unable to unearth any information at all. If, however, you have any details to add to their story, I will of course be extremely grateful.

The first soldier is, of course, my grandfather Mervyn Berry whose records first inspired me to write this book. The following chapters are written with surnames in alphabetical order rather than chronological to make it easier for the reader to find their man and also because it is their story and therefore individual.

Several men served in the same regiment and battalion. For instance, Frank Bartlett, Arthur Cyphus and Fred Vellender were all in the 12th Battalion Hampshire Regiment. This means their stories intertwine. I have included different War Diary extracts for them to make their stories more individual, but they often apply to all the men in that battalion. There is some repetition regarding places, dates and events. This is deliberate because I want the chapters to be entire and also readers will not have to refer back if they only want to read about one or two men.

Mervyn Berry

53916 Private H. M. Berry Machine Gun Corps

(HARRY) MERVYN BERRY was born on 19 September 1897, at Waterbank, Great Rissington, to Harry and Clara Berry nee Smith. His father was a Master Baker at The Bakehouse and his mother ran the village Post Office along with his sister Kitty.

In 1915, Mervyn signed up under the Derby Scheme at Stow on the Wold. Mervyn signed his papers on 11 December 1915 and afterwards went home to work in his father's bakery until he was called up.

He was mobilised for service on 21 June 1916, when he was still only 18 years old, joining the 11th (Reserve) Battalion Gloucestershire Regiment. The battalion was based in Seaford, Sussex and here Mervyn did his basic training including physical fitness, drill, marching and rifle practice.

Mervyn's hut at Seaford Camp

On 21 August 1916, Mervyn was transferred to the 81st Brigade Machine Gun Company, which was part of the 27th Division. The Machine Gun Corps (MGC) was formed in October 1915, with infantry, cavalry and motor branches, and in early 1916 a heavy branch, too. The training centre for the MGC was established at Belton Park in Grantham, Lincolnshire. Existing battalion machine gun sections transferred to the MGC and other men were enlisted or transferred directly into it. It was at Grantham that Mervyn was trained to use a Vickers machine gun.

The Vickers machine gun was fired from a tripod and cooled by water held in a jacket around the barrel. The gun weighed over 28lbs, the tripod 20lbs and the water to cool it a further 20lbs. The bullets came in a canvas belt, which held 250 rounds. A Vickers gun team comprised of six men, which included the gunner, one man to feed the ammunition and four to carry the equipment.

In 'With a Machine Gun to Cambrai' (1969), George Coppard, explains how the Vickers gun team worked.

> "Number One was leader and fired the gun, while Number Two controlled the entry of ammo belts into the feed-block.

Number Three maintained a supply of ammo to Number Two, and Number Four to Six were reserves and carriers, but all the members of the team were fully trained in handling the gun."

Mervyn completed his training on the Vickers gun and on 26 October 1916 left England from Southampton for Camiers in France, which was the base depot of the MGC. In her diary, Mervyn's mother Clara recorded;

"Mervyn went to France 26th October 1916".

After further training in Camiers on the Vickers gun, Mervyn was posted to Salonika, travelling via Marseilles and arriving in December 1916. The initial Franco-British force's objective was to assist the Serbs against Bulgarian hostilities but they arrived too late. Despite Greek opposition, the troops were kept in Salonika for future operations, in a camp known as 'The Birdcage'.

The soldiers in Salonika were known in Britain as the 'Gardeners of Salonika' owing to all the digging that the men undertook and a noticeable lack of activity. It was said, *"If you want a holiday, go to Salonika".* Over the first few months, Mervyn spent most of his time preparing gun emplacements, putting out belts of wire and practicing firing the Vickers gun along the Struma Valley. He also went on a bombing course.

Mervyn in Salonika

War Diaries 81st Brigade Machine Gun Company

01.07.1917
Wire being put up for the 2 guns covering KOMARJAN BRIDGEHEAD.

01.07.1917
Two emplacements started on right bank of STRUMA to fire up this wire.

03.07.1917
Emplacements almost completed. Guns moved into them.

04.07.1917
Instruction in bombing begun. Officers and NCO's to have a thorough knowledge; men to be able to throw only.

Despite this quiet front, the British Salonika Force had to cope with extremes in temperature, sand-fly fever, dysentery and malaria. Malaria was endemic in Salonika and on 21 July 1917, Mervyn reported sick and was admitted to Number 27 Casualty Clearing Station (CCS) suffering from this condition. It is estimated that 83% of The British Salonika Force were infected with malaria. Symptoms included a high temperature, headaches and shivering, similar to flu. Repeated attacks can be debilitating and many men were left feeling weak. Quinine was available which was taken to prevent as well as to treat infection with hospitalised men receiving it intravenously.

When Mervyn returned to duty he spent a few days at the base depot in Salonika, to get back into the swing of things, before rejoining his machine gun company in the field. During the rest of 1917, the 81st MGC occupied Kristian Kamila defences, moving their guns to different positions and at night firing on the enemy practicing for an attack. The men were sleeping in bivouacs, which helped prevent so much sickness from sand-fly fever. In mid September, the 81st MGC took part in a machine gun competition against the 82nd MGC, which they won.

War Diaries 81st Brigade Machine Gun Company

20.09.1917
Military Events M.G. Competition between this Company and the 82nd M.G.Coy taken place. The 80th M.G.Coy did not enter owing to the long distance they had to travel. The G.O.C., 81st Inf. Bde. were present. 81st M.G.Coy won on total points by 14, getting 302 out of a possible 500. The 82nd M.G.Coy scored 288 points.

On 25 October 1917, Mervyn was once again suffering from malaria and was admitted to hospital where he stayed until 6 November 1917. After a further period at the base depot he rejoined his company in the New Year at Sakavca in the Struma Valley. Mervyn tested his gas mask by entering gas chambers with the rest of his company.

War Diaries 81st Brigade Machine Gun Company

10.01.1918
All the Company, with the exception of the men in the line to be put through a Gas Chamber, near SAKAVCA. 2/Lieut Templeton admitted to hospital with fever. Promulgation of Courts Marshall

12.01.1918
All men in the line are relieved for the day and put through the Gas Chamber.

Mervyn was sent on a Signallers Course on 27 June 1918. Here he learnt semaphore, hand and arm signals and visual training for long and short distances. It was important to be able to give and receive signals with Vickers gun crews spread so far apart. On 1 September 1918, Mervyn took part in an offensive to capture the Roche Noire Salient. This was a piece of land that jutted out in front of the Bulgarian lines. It was heavily fortified with a ravine running through the centre, machine gun emplacements and triple belts of barbed wire. The attack would take place at 5.30pm with the infantry rushing across with no warning by artillery barrage.

The MG Company's operation orders for the attack issued the following instructions:

Fighting Kit

The following will be worn or carried. All Officers in the fighting line are to be dressed and equipped exactly like the rank & file with the following exceptions.

Badges of rank will be worn on the shoulders
Revolvers will be carried
For all ranks the haversack and waterproof sheet will be carried on the back.
One iron ration and mess tin in the haversack, water bottle full
2 Bombs will be carried in the top pocket of the jacket by every man. These will be issued at forming up places and on arrival at new positions if not required will be handed over to O.C. gun team
Box respirators will be carried and Helmets P.G.H.
Packs will be stored in Officers or other shelters in present frontline under charge of the reserve guns.
Rations: A hot meal will be provided at the forming up positions prior to the assault, thereafter until further arrangements are made, Officers Commanding subsections and teams in the captured positions will arrange to be rationed by the nearest Infantry Coy.

Even in the heat of battle, machine gun teams were expected to carry a full pack and equipment as well as their Vickers gun, tripod and ammunition belts. A total of 170,000 officers and men served in the Machine Gun Corps. With over 62,000 becoming casualties, including 12,498 being killed.

A further attack of malaria on 5 October 1918 caused Mervyn to be admitted to No. 50 General Hospital. When the Armistice on the Western Front was announced, Mervyn was at the Brigade Base Depot in Salonika. It would be quite a while before the war was over for him. He returned to his company on 23 November 1918 and continued with his duties.

On 19 December 1918, Mervyn left the camp without permission and managed to lose his service revolver. He opted to be dealt with by his Commanding Officer rather than by Court Marshall and on 20 December 1918 he was brought before Second Lieutenant Vanstone for the offence of *'Breaking out of camp and losing by neglect his revolver'*. Mervyn was found to be guilty and punished with 28 days Field Punishment Number 1 (FP No. 1) and had to pay £1-15-6d towards the cost of his revolver.

FP No. 1 consisted of the convicted man being placed in shackles or restraints and attached to a fixed object such as a gun wheel or post for two hours a day, on 3 days out of 4. It was usually applied in field punishment camps set up for this purpose a few miles behind the frontline, but when the unit was on the move the unit itself would carry it out.

Four days later on Christmas Eve, Mervyn was posted to the North Russia Expeditionary Force (NREF). The NREF was part of the Allied Intervention in Russia after the October Revolution. The revolution divided the people into Red Russians who were communists and White Russians who wanted democracy. In spring 1918, Lenin signed a peace treaty with Germany, in order to gain time. In South Russia and the Ukraine, the British gave military support to the White forces under General Denikin to help stamp out Bolshevism.

Mervyn embarked on the S.S.Ellenga and passed down the Gallipoli coast and the Dardanelles during the voyage arriving at Constantinople, known as Constant during the war, on 28 December 1918.

The ship docked at Constantinople to take on supplies and then sailed through the Bosphorous to the Black Sea arriving in Batoum on 30 December 1918.

War Diaries 81st Brigade Machine Gun Company

31.12.1918
BATOUM
Disembarked at 1200 hours and marched to the Russian Barracks where Coy was quartered. The officers were quartered in the Wireless Station. All ranks warned not to accept English Leaseway Notes from the inhabitants, as they were Turkish forgeries.

01.01.19
Cleaned guns and equipment

Mervyn spent nine days in Batoum cleaning guns and equipment and training. The Horse Transport arrived on 6 January 1919 with all horses and mules in good condition. On 9 January 1919, Mervyn travelled by train for a 200 mile journey inland to Tiflis, the capital of Georgia. The Company were billeted in the girl's school where every man had an iron bedstead. Mervyn and the 81st Brigade spent the next few weeks building stables to house the horses and mules for the winter. The weather was cold and snowy.

War Diaries 81st Brigade Machine Gun Company

01.02.1919
TIFLIS
Cold chilly weather. Letter from Capt Bruce asking to be applied for as he is being delayed at G.B.D. SALONIKA. Attempt to come to some agreement with Director of school about furniture etc. but find him very unsatisfactory; nothing definite arranged. Election going on in GEORGIA. 14 parties numbered 1 to 14. Nos 1 and 3 said to be "Bolshevists" and fears expressed that they may get in. No 2 party appear to be the strongest. Rouble (GEORGIAN) unofficially fixed at 80 to £1 which is fairly reasonable. Eggs cost 1.20py a bit over 3d½ each. A tea at Frasentis anything from 30pys. Snow started falling about 2100 hrs. Mules go into stables which hold 136 easy.

By 11 February 1919, the company had been *'kicked out of our comfy billet'* by the 18th Stationary Hospital. Mervyn marched to the new barracks in four inches of snow with more falling steadily all day. There were no beds and he spent the night lying on the concrete floor. There were rumours of anti-British demonstrations in Tiflis and the company manned the guns in readiness for any trouble.

The British Army were needed to guard the 500 miles of oil wells along the railway line between Baku and Batoum. Disease was rife in the area and many men were hospitalised, including Mervyn who went sick in May, eventually being transferred back to Constantinople on the S.S. Glancome Castle. He never returned to duty in Tiflis and on 28 November 1919 he was shipped back home to Fovant in England where he was demobilised.

After the war Mervyn went home to Great Rissington, working alongside his father Harry once more in the bakery. He married Edie (Edith) Hovard in 1922 and they went on to have seven sons, one of whom, Leonard, front row right, is my father.

Mervyn, Edie and their boys

During World War Two, Mervyn worked at the Gloucester Aircraft Company in Brockworth as an airframe fitter on the Gloster Meteor. He was also a member of the Home Guard in Great Rissington.

It is well known in the family that Mervyn was a very talented man who could turn his hand to most things. During his war service in Salonika, he had to contend with disease as well as trying to 'dodge the bullets'. For every casualty of war in Salonika, three actually died of malaria, influenza or other sickness. Mervyn survived the

Mervyn, (4th left, 2nd row) with some of the Gloster Meteor team

First World War, against the odds, only to die, aged just 52, from Tetanus, a preventable disease today. He is buried in St John the Baptist Churchyard Extension in Great Rissington.

Frank Bartlett

13805 Corporal F H Bartlett Hampshire Regiment

FRANCIS HARRY BARTLETT was born in Great Rissington in 1893, the eldest son of George Bartlett and Margaret (nee Cyphus). Frank lived with his parents and his sisters Winifred born 1897 and Doris born 1900 and a younger brother Reginald born 1903. He worked as a Farm Labourer at Rissington Hill Farm for Richard Bolter.

When Kitchener called for volunteers to increase the army, Frank enlisted into the Hampshire Regiment at Bourton on the Water and joined the 12th (Service) Battalion, 'B' Company on 5 September 1914, one month after the outbreak of the war.

Frank Mills, Arthur Cyphus and Fred Vellender also joined the 12th Hampshires and they would serve together during the war. Frank sailed from Southampton on 20 September 1915 and arrived in Le Havre, France the following day. After a further 10 days training, the battalion moved into trenches at Cachy on 8 October to initiate the men in frontline duties and to allow them to learn the ropes from more experienced troops. Frank spent the next months rotating between the frontline, reserve trenches and training at base camp in physical fitness, drill and march discipline. Troops usually spent four days in frontline trenches, four in support, four in reserve and then have a period of rest at a base camp nearby before starting the cycle all over again.

The 12th Hampshire Battalion was selected to go to Salonika in Greece and on 11 November 1915 Frank embarked on the S.S.

Canada sailing to Salonika via Alexandria arriving on 25 November 1915.

In October 1915, Bulgaria attacked Serbia and the Serbs appealed for military assistance. At the same time, Greece also asked the allies for help because they had a treaty with Serbia. The British and French decided to send 150,000 men from France to help them. They advanced into Macedonia but were too late and retreated back to Salonika, set up camp and prepared the port for defence.

Frank had already been promoted to Lance Corporal and in January 1916 he was further promoted to Corporal. He was also granted Proficiency Pay Class II (PPII). Proficiency pay meant another 6d a day for Frank. It is not known why he was awarded this but PPII was usually given because of a special skill or because of rank or promotion.

On 1 October 1916, Frank was unlucky and went down with dysentery, which had broken out amongst the troops that summer. He was admitted to 43rd General Hospital Salonika for treatment, which started with an initial purge of castor oil followed by doses of saline four times a day. The hospital was 80 miles from the front and consisted of rows and rows of wooden huts and tents. There were about 2,000 beds in all and the men could hear aircraft flying overhead and the sound of the guns in the distance.

Frank spent a week in the hospital and was then evacuated via the Hospital Ship Herefordshire to Imtarfa Hospital in Malta, where he arrived on 10 October 1916. He was to spend some months here recuperating and was invalided to England aboard the Hospital Ship Asturias in March 1917. The Asturias was the largest hospital ship afloat; about 12,000 tonnes. The cabins were knocked out and in their place were huge wards filled with beds.

A few days after Frank arrived in England, the Asturias was torpedoed off the Devonshire coast, on the 21 March, but was only damaged. Although it was not carrying patients at the time, 41 people lost their lives.

After Frank had recovered from dysentery he was posted back to the front. He embarked at Southampton on 13 June 1917 and arrived in France the following day at No 3 Infantry Base Depot at Rouen where he did some training preparatory to returning to the frontline. He then left for Salonika and rejoined the 12th Hampshires, where he continued with his duties.

Frank seemed destined to spend his war in a hospital bed because he caught influenza on 22 July 1917 and found himself back at Rouen in No 6 General Hospital. Spanish Flu spread rapidly around the world in 1918 and between 20 and 40 million people are estimated to have died from it worldwide. Frank was also diagnosed with pyrexia (or Trench Fever), which eventually turned out to be malaria. He was shipped back home to Blighty to recover. The vast majority of patients were suffering from malaria, the most endemic medical problem in Salonika, which was spread through mosquito bites.

Frank survived the flu but didn't return to the front. He stayed in England with the 4th (Res) Hampshires in Gosport, where he remained until the end of the war on home defence duty.

When the Armistice was declared, Frank moved to a dispersal area at Chiseldon, near Swindon. In January 1919 he was examined by the Battalion Medical Officer when he applied for a pension. The medical officer noted;

> 'He has lost some weight but is now improving. He is slightly debilitated'

He was awarded a pension for six months owing to his malaria and returned home to Great Rissington on 12 March 1919. Later, Frank moved to Birmingham to work as a guard on the railways. He married Elsie Bartlett in 1927 and was living in Solihull when he died aged 80.

The Bolter Boys

FREDERICK SAMUEL AND Thomas William, known as Fred and Will, were born at Hilmarton, Wiltshire in 1894 and 1896, where their father, Richard Bolter, managed Catcomb Farm. In around 1898, Richard and his wife Emily moved to Great Rissington with their children and Richard's parents. The extended family took over the tenancy of Rissington Hill Farm. Two further children had been born at Hilmarton, Reg and Mary and a fourth son, Cyril was born in Great Rissington, but died aged two.

Rissington Hill stocked animals such as sheep, cattle, pigs and horses as well as having arable fields of wheat and barley. Fred and Will's father specialised in breeding and showing Shire Horses, calling them names such as, *Rissington Poppy* and *Rissington Jewel*.

When Great Britain declared war on Germany in August 1914, Fred and Will were both working on the farm in partnership

From left to right, Will, Reg, Mary and Fred

Rissington Hill Farm c1910, glimpsed through the trees far left

with their father. Richard Bolter employed a lot of village men and boys on the farm and was an active member of the Church and one of the managers of the Board School.

Fred Bolter

2700 Private F S Bolter Berkshire Yeomanry

FRED JOINED THE Berkshire Yeomanry in late May/early June 1915 at Yeomanry House, Reading, where he was interviewed by Sergeant Clifford and passed as A1 fit. After taking the King's Shilling he was issued with a uniform and a railway warrant to proceed to Aldermaston, Berkshire. Here he began his training with the 3/1st Berkshire Yeomanry and after passing out was sent to Tidworth, Wiltshire to finish his cavalry training. As Fred was a Farmer's son he was a suitable recruit for the Yeomanry because he could already ride and owned his own horse.

Frustratingly, the War Diaries of the Berkshire Yeomanry were lost but Fred most likely sailed with the first draft of 100 men that left England in October 1915 for Alexandria. Here, in December 1915, the Berkshire Yeomanry started to re-fit as cavalry. Fred would probably have been issued with his horse by the Army, or he may have taken his own horse with him. The Berkshire Yeomanry had taken part in the attacks against the Turks at Suvla Bay, Gallipoli in August the same year and had suffered massive losses. After three months in the trenches, the Regiment was withdrawn, their strength reduced by casualties and sickness to a mere 50 men. In October they left Gallipoli and headed for Egypt.

The Regiment was bought up to strength in December 1915 at Mena Camp, Egypt. This was a huge hut and tent city based in the grounds of Mena House, a large hotel near the Pyramids. The hotel itself was used as a hospital during the war. As a mounted soldier, Fred saw service in the Sinai Peninsula and in Palestine in 1916. In 1917, Fred joined the British advance on Jerusalem. After two unsuccessful battles to evict the Turkish Army from Gaza, the British forces were reorganised under their new commander General Allenby and during the third Battle of Gaza in December 1917 they captured Jerusalem. During this campaign the Berkshire Yeomanry were involved in two successful cavalry charges against the Turks.

In April 1918, the Regiment was amalgamated into 101st (Buckinghamshire & Berkshire Yeomanry) Battalion, Machine Gun Corps and posted to the Western Front. On Thursday, 23 May 1918, Fred boarded the Leasowe Castle, which was torpedoed by a German submarine, (UB51) and sunk. A survivor of the sinking gave this account:

> "The 'Leasowe Castle' was one of a convoy of six transporters and they were accompanied by a number of destroyers. The weather was good, the sea was calm and a brilliant moon shone in the night sky. At 1.30 am on 27 May 1918, when the ship was about 104 miles from Alexandria, the 'Leasowe Castle' was struck by a torpedo on the starboard side. The engines were immediately stopped. The troops mustered to their stations, rolls were called, boats lowered and rafts flung overboard. The Japanese destroyer 'R' stood by, while the remainder of the convoy continued on their journey at full speed. We are informed that perfect order was maintained on board, the men standing quietly at their stations as if on parade, while those detailed for the work assisted in lowering the boats. Lifeboats were launched in the course of forty five minutes and the rescue attempt continued smoothly. The 'Leasowe Castle' remained fairly steady, though sinking a little at the stern, with a slight list to port. About 1.45am, HM sloop 'Lily' appeared, having turned back from the convoy to assist in the work of rescue. She ran her bows up to the starboard side of the 'Leasowe Castle' and made fast, so that troops were able to pass quickly on board. Meanwhile the Japanese destroyer put up a smoke screen for protection.

Suddenly, about 3.00 am, a bulkhead in the aft part of the ship gave way, and with a loud noise the 'Leasowe Castle' sank rapidly. The 'Lily' had a narrow escape, as the hawsers connecting her with the sinking ship were cut with an axe just in time."

Fred was one of the lucky ones and survived the sinking. He eventually arrived in Etaples, France in July. Later he moved to Belgium and took part in the final battles of Arras in August, Ypres in September and the October advance to the Rhine.

After the war he returned to Great Rissington and his father set him up at a farm at Lower Harford. He married Wynifred Perry and they had two children, Dennis and Jean. Fred died in 1978. He can be seen in the demob photo kneeling second on the left.

Will Bolter

46089 Private T W Bolter Leicestershire Regiment

WILL JOINED THE 11th (Service) Battalion Leicestershire Regiment, (The Leicester Tigers), sometime in 1916. The 11th Leicesters was a Pioneer battalion attached to the 6th Division.

One solution for the huge demand for labour was the creation of a labour battalion for each infantry division. These men would be trained as infantry but would be deployed on labouring tasks. They were called Pioneers and were composed of men who had experience with picks and shovels and had skilled trades, such as miners, joiners, bricklayers and fitters. Pioneer battalions were responsible for constructing trenches and they often consolidated these trenches in the heat of battle. The 11th Leicesters were also known as the Midland Pioneers.

In March 1916, Will was still in Leicester at the base depot learning the ropes of a soldier's life. On the 9 March, the battalion received orders to mobilise but they still had no rifles, machine guns or any ammunition. The equipment started to arrive over the next few days and on the 17 March 64 mules were delivered and had to be billeted in various stables in the town. By the 23 March the battalion was at last on the move for France.

War Diaries, 11th (Service) Battalion Leicestershire Regiment

25.3.1916
2.30am Commenced entraining transport.
6.50am Battalion entrained in three trains for Southampton via Banbury and Basingstoke.

Will was part of the transport section and his train arrived at Southampton at 11.15pm.

He boarded HMT Rossetti and then spent the night aboard ship as it waited in the docks. The weather was very rough and so at 9.00am the men were sent on a route march to kill time before they sailed. At 3pm Will once again boarded HM Rossetti and set off for Le Havre, France. The remainder of the battalion embarked on HMT Pancras and HMT Marguarite at 6pm. Owing to the bad weather, the Marguarite and the Rossetti were compelled to turn back to Southampton but the troops remained on board. The Pancras managed to carry on and the troops disembarked at 5pm and marched off to a rest camp. The rest of the battalion arrived the following day at 1am. After the rough crossing, the men were allowed to rest for two days before marching to the railway station at Marchandises. Here, Will was to see at first hand how troops were transported on the French railways.

Will astride a horse

THE BOLTER BOYS

War Diaries, 11th (Service) Battalion Leicestershire Regiment

31.3.1916
Entrained at GARE DES MARCHANDISES. Sheepskin coats, gloves and felt socks issued for journey

The rank and file travelled in closed cattle trucks with a little straw on the floor. Each truck was marked with the words, HOMMES 40, CHEVAUX 8. As it wasn't clear whether the men and horses got in together, Will may well have been relieved to be packed into a truck along with 39 other men. Space was minimal, with the men jam packed with their equipment and no room to relax. The trains generally travelled at about 5mph and soldiers could get off to stretch their legs and buy provisions along the way.

The train arrived at Hazebrouck in Belgium at 7.30pm and one man was immediately sent to hospital suffering from meningitis. The rest of the battalion had to march for an hour till they reached Poperinge. Poperinge, known as 'Pop' to the British Tommy, was the town most soldiers passed through on their way to Ypres. Despite being shelled and bombed daily, many men regarded it as a haven where they could buy souvenirs, treats and get a decent meal, such as egg and chips. Poperinge also housed the 'Every Man's Club' called Talbot House or Toc H, which was run by an Army Chaplain called Philip 'Tubby' Clayton and where all men were welcome. Caps were handed in at the door and all ranks were treated the same.

Over the next few days, more men were hospitalised with meningitis and one was admitted for being mentally deranged. The men were also obliged to hand in their sheepskin coats to the quartermaster stores.

Will was to spend some months in Ypres where the 11th Leicesters dug new trenches, acted as carrying parties and did general duties. Keeping roads and trenches in good order was a hazardous job, as quoted from J. Cumming Morgan's Memoirs and Diaries: A Labour Company at Ypres, (1930).

> "Forward the "Labour Corps!" A squad of men is quickly on the spot with pick and shovel, and the hole is filled up with

any mortal thing that can be found - stones, beams, bricks, railway lines, sleepers, bits of cars or lorries, wheels, cases of bully, tombstones, dead horses - anything that will occupy space, and in a few minutes the traffic moves on once more, and the War goes on!"

In July 1917, the 11th Leicesters became attached to the 7th Battalion Canadian Railway Troops at Dickebusche. The Canadian Railway Battalions constructed light railways and extensive tramways in the Ypres sector during the war. Operation orders for Will's battalion were as follows;

War Diaries, 11th (Service) Battalion Leicestershire Regiment

30.7 1917
1. The Battalion will be disposed near Dickebusche for Light Railway construction from today as follows:
    C Coy working with B Coy on Grading
    A Coy working with D Coy on Track Laying
    B and D Coys working with C Coy on Ballasting

2. On Zero day, which will be notified later, the Battalion will hold itself in readiness to move forward for work on Light Railways. Packs will be left behind at the present camp. Fifty rounds of ammunition per man will be carried; the remainder will be handed in to Quarter Masters Stores immediately on receipt of this order. Every man under the rank of Sergeant will carry a shovel.

3. It is proposed to establish a bivouac for the Grading, Track laying and ballasting detachments on the North side of Zillebeke Lake on "Z" night. Allotments of ground space will be reserved by the Quarter Master 7th C.R.T. and will be notified later.

4. Water will be carried up in petrol tins, fifty tins per company are being issued and no water from these is to be used for any other purpose than drinking.

5. A small party will be left behind in the present camp to look after surplus stores etc. The transport section will also remain behind, and separate orders will be issued later with reference to their movement. The Quarter Master and the Interpreter will remain behind with the transport.

6. Officers will endeavour to reduce their kits and Mess kits as far as possible, all spare kits being left with the Quarter Master.

7. A Field Headquarters will be established by the 7th Battalion Canadian Railway Troops, the location of which will be notified later.

H M Raleigh Capt & Adjt
11th Leicestershire Regt (Pioneers)

Canadian Railway Troops (CRT) laid steel tracks to the forward trenches to bring up stores and ammunition, and repaired breaks in the lines caused by heavy German shellfire. The Third Battle of *Passchendaele* was underway and the railways were continuously shelled by the enemy. CRT had only basic training for frontline work and did not have the protection of trenches. The weather was dreadful with heavy rain turning the ground into a swamp. In this hellish atmosphere the 11th Leicesters carried out their work alongside the Canadians.

It was probably during this time that Will suffered the serious wounds that caused him to be invalided out of the army. He returned to his father's farm in Great Rissington and can be seen on the demob photo taken in 1919 kneeling third right. Will wasn't a well man and he eventually died from the effects of his wounds on 10 August 1919 aged just 23. He is buried in St John the Baptist's Churchyard Extension, Great Rissington and his photo is also displayed in the church.

Joe Cambray

39541 Private J H Cambray York and Lancaster Regiment

JOSEPH HENRY CAMBRAY was born in Great Rissington in 1896. He was the youngest son of Henry and Elizabeth Cambray (nee Davis). Henry Cambray was a Slater and Plasterer, running his own business. The Cambray family name is one of the oldest in the village.

Joe left school aged 14 to work as a milk carrier for his uncle, Richard Davis, who owned a dairy in Cheltenham. Joe lodged with the family at 3, Rotunda Terrace in Montpellier.

In July 1915, aged 19, Joe attested at Gloucester and enlisted into the Army Cyclists Corps, D Company. At his medical, he was shown to be *'5ft 5" tall, 138lbs, chest 42" with an expansion of 3½'*. He must have had an exceptional chest, because the Doctor called all his colleagues in to the room to see his *'perfect physique'*. (As related by Joe, to his Godson, Leonard Berry.)

Whilst still at training camp in Cheltenham, Joe was brought before Captain Talbot-Plum. He had been *'absent from Tattoo till found in billet, Reveille, 27th October 1916'*, and found by his Sergeant. His offence was given as *'drunkenness'* and he was punished with a forfeit of *'one day's pay'* and *'confined to barracks one day'*.

Joe was transferred to the York and Lancaster Regiment on 23 Nov 1916, based at Chisleden, a hutted camp near Swindon, and then posted to France. He joined the 8th Battalion at Etaples on New Year's Eve 1916. This training camp in France was notorious for its tough regime and known as 'The Bull Ring'. Within three days of his arrival in France, Joe was once again transferred to the 6th Battalion and was billeted at Prouville in the Somme region, resting, re-clothing and re-equipping. Towards the middle of January, Joe moved to the front at Beaucourt sur l'Ancre, an area that had seen fierce fighting during the battle of the Somme. Beaucourt was eventually taken in November 1916 by the 63rd Royal Naval Division. This division was composed mainly of surplus reserves of the Royal Navy who were not required at sea. Joe's battalion relieved the 6th Yorkshire Regiment in the frontline trenches at Beaucourt on the 14th January 1917.

Beaucourt sur l'Ancre station in 2005

War Diaries 6th (Service) Battalion York and Lancaster Regiment

15.1.1917
Ordinary trench routine.

16.1.1917
Details received for attack on enemy outposts.

17.1.1917
4am H.Q. moved to SUVLA TRENCH.
6.55am Battn. attacked enemy outpost line. All objectives were gained by 7.30am. Consolidation was successfully carried out during day and night. Casualties: <u>Killed</u> *1 Officer, 9 O.R.,* <u>Wounded</u> *5 Officers, 92 O.R.,* <u>Missing</u> *12 O.R.*

18.1.1917
4.30pm Outposts project forward about 200 yards and a strong point was made at junction of ARTILLERY ALLEY and PUISIEUX ROAD. Battn. relieved by 63rd (R.N.) Division, relief completed by 12.35am.

After a period in reserve trenches, Joe moved to the rear for some rest and a bath. The battalion then left the Ancre valley and moved north towards Cambrai. Cambrai was an important railhead behind German lines with two lines of concrete fortifications and a 10 yards wide barbed wire belt in front of it. This was known as the Hindenburg Line and the Germans had withdrawn to this in the spring of 1917.

War Diaries 6th (Service) Battalion York and Lancaster Regiment

24.4.1917
Battn. at DEMICOURT, took over Frontline trenches from 3rd Australian Infantry, relief successfully accomplished.

25.4.1917
Ordinary trench routine, enemy was quiet and showed us his position to draw our fire. His shelling was intermittent and chiefly on villages.

28.4.1917
We launched a gas attack onto Lock 7, CANAL DU NORD, followed by gas shell bombardment at 2.40am. Enemy's reply was very feeble; practically no MG or rifle fire & artillery barrage did not open till zero + 35. Our casualties from this were nil. Rest of the day was quiet.

30.4.1917
Quiet day, practically no shelling. Battn. relieved by 9/West Yorkshires, relief quietly and successfully accomplished. Battn. went into support at BEAUMETZ LES CAMBRAI in bivouacs. Total casualties for month 2 OR killed, 1 OR died of wounds, 3 OR wounded. Total reinforcements, 3 Officers, 62 OR

On 30 May 1917, Joe's unit was attached to 299 Siege Battery Royal Garrison Artillery (RGA). 299 Siege Battery were part of the 85 Heavy Artillery Group with a 4 x 6 inch howitzer (26 cwt) battery. The battery may have needed men who knew the terrain and asked for volunteers to assist the Forward Observation Officer of the battery in directing the attack on Messines and pinpointing the creeping barrage over the first few days of June. This was a very dangerous job, spotting potential targets and observing the effects of their firing. Joe's battalion was no doubt in the thick of it, taking part in the assault. The attack began on 3rd June when the preliminary bombardment was intensified and kept up till the 7th June when 19 mines exploded under the enemy lines. The blast killed over 6000 Germans with 10,000 missing. It was so loud it was heard by Lloyd George, the British Prime Minister, who was in his study at Downing Street in London. Nine divisions of infantry advanced and the Messines Ridge was taken within three hours.

War Diaries 229 Siege Battery Royal Garrison Artillery

1.6.1917
350 rounds on enemy trenches

2.6.1917
480 rounds on enemy trenches. Bombardment. 120 rounds on MESSINES.

4.6.1917
281 rounds on wire cutting and machine gun emplacement.

5.6.1917
8.45am 200 rounds wire cutting on two points ranged by aeroplane.
    3pm 80 rounds demonstration barrage. Blind shoot.
    3.30pm 325 rounds on 5 O.P's – 65 rounds on each.
    10.20pm 114 rounds on Trench junctions in support raid by Royal Inniskillings.

7.6.1917
1347 rounds on Bombardment. Various targets allotted. Very satisfactory. WYSCHAETE MESINES Ridge taken by 2nd Army.

JOE CAMBRAY

On the 9 June the battery pulled out and proceeded to Poperinge for a rest period. They had endured heavy shelling, gas attacks, wounded and killed men, direct hits and had one gun completely knocked out during the seven days of bombardment. Joe spent June and July with the RGA before returning to his battalion. The 6th Yorks and Lancs had been through a tough time during the Battle of Messines and the total casualties for the month of June were 203 wounded, shell shocked and killed.

Joe later took part in part in the battle of Cambrai in November/December 1917. This was the first battle in which tanks were used in large numbers. 350 tanks advanced across no man's land supported by the infantry and covered by a rolling barrage of artillery.

The attack took the Germans completely by surprise and the Third Army gained over five miles in the first day. On the 30 November the Germans launched a counter-attack and by the time the battle came to an end on 7 December, they had regained almost all the ground taken at the start. During the fighting, the British suffered over 44,000 casualties, killed, wounded and missing and the German losses were estimated in the region of 45,000.

The York and Lancaster Regiment raised 22 battalions during the war and out of every 100 men, 72 were either wounded or killed. Joe was fortunate and only had one minor wound during the war when some shrapnel hit a finger. He returned home to his family in Great Rissington, along with an advance of £2 pay and was officially demobilised on 8 March the same year.

Joe married Lilian Crockford in 1927 and they had two daughters, Betty and Mabel. He worked for Great Western Railways at Bourton on the Water station as a deliveryman after the war and can be seen in the demob photo seated second left and in the village parade photo, where he is carrying the British Legion Flag. He died in 1954 aged 58 and is buried in St John the Baptist's Churchyard Extension, Great Rissington.

Arthur Cyphus

13208 Sergeant A Cyphus Hampshire Regiment

ARTHUR CYPHUS WAS born in Great Rissington in 1888, and was the son of Robert Cyphus and Rachel (nee Webley). He was one of seven children and in 1901 was working as a delivery boy for Tom Smith who lived in The Yews and had a butchers shop. Arthur joined the 12th (Service) Battalion Hampshire Regiment, part of the 26th Division, which was the last division to be formed for the Third New Army (K3). In September 1915 Arthur sailed from Southampton for Le Havre, France.

In November 1915, Arthur and his battalion were in billets at Beaucourt sur L'Ancre in France. Where Joe Cambray would be fighting two years later. The weather was very wet and bitterly cold. Here various training sessions took place including entrenching, fatigues and musketry. On the 10 November, the battalion was posted to Salonika. Arthur packed up his kit and entrained at Longeau, spending two days travelling to Marseille and a further 10 days at sea aboard S.S. Canada.

It was a calm journey but it was pouring with rain when he disembarked. From the port, he marched three miles to camp and went into billets where he received dry clothes and a hot meal.

Arthur continued his training under unrelentingly harsh weather conditions. During January, there were heavy snowfalls, blizzards and it was freezing cold. He spent most of his time over the next year doing route marches, musketry drill and digging miles and miles of trench works.

On 7 January 1916, German air raids caused 18 casualties and Zeppelins caused damage and fires during February. There was a further Zeppelin raid on 27 March.

War Diaries 12th (Service) Battalion Hampshire Regiment

27.3.16
ROBINSONS MULLAH
Zeppelin and aeroplane raid at 5am. All quiet on our front. Weather fine. Work continued cutting stakes, preparing wire obstacles, deepening trenches, cutting down bushes & cleaning ground.

The Zeppelin raid caused a lot of damage and the French stores were hit. When it appeared again on 5 May it was caught in the searchlights of H.M.S. Agamemnon and brought down into the river Vadar. A propeller from the Zeppelin was presented to H.M.S. Agamemnon and hung in the Captain's cabin.

At Christmas that year the battalion celebrated with a church parade in the morning, which the C.O. noted as being a *'Very enjoyable day.'* The men had their Christmas dinner followed by entertainment in the afternoon.

In April 1917, the battalion were to take part in an attack on the enemy lines. The weeks leading up to the attack were spent in practice sessions against other battalions. Here they covered physical drill, close order drill, bayonet fighting, bombing, extended order drill and artillery formation. They also had to suffer a long lecture from the C.O. in weather that was very warm but wet. However, there was also time for the battalion to enjoy a game of football.

War Diaries 12th (Service) Battalion Hampshire Regiment

19.4.1917
Football match against City of London Yeomanry. Win 4-1

On the 23 April the 12th Hampshires were striking tents and cleaning the camp. That night they moved to Deep Cut Ravine camp and the following day at 4pm, moved through the communication trenches to their forming up positions at Minden and Silbury Support Camp. The following operation orders were read out to the men in preparation for the battle. Even in the heat of battle, men were expected to carry extra equipment to consolidate their position after an attack.

War Diaries 12th (Service) Battalion Hampshire Regiment

Operation orders
To attack and occupy the enemy's advanced works from the LAKE to JUMEAUX RAVINE inclusive Fighting kit
The following will be worn or carried
  A pick or shovel will be carried by every man. To be carried on the back under the haversack, the head of the tool resting on the top. A haversack and waterproof sheet, iron rations, mess-tin and water bottles, full.
  Three sandbags will be carried by every man
  170 round and two bombs in the top pocket by every man
  Gas helmets
  Coloured flags – two per platoon
  Wire cutters and breakers
  Periscopes

At 8.15pm, Arthur with his battalion moved to the assembly positions in Y Ravine, Jumeaux Ravine and Sunken Road. Some companies were unable to reach their positions before the attack. Arthur was in the first wave of the assault. It was to be a night assault with an artillery bombardment used to soften the enemy's defences. However, the Bulgarians controlled the heights and could see the troop build-up. They fired shells all along the Jumeaux Ravine causing hold ups and congestion. By the early hours of the 25 April the trenches were full of dead and dying men. Many officers and NCO's were killed leaving the Hampshires to return to their start point at the trenches they had set off from. The battalion had almost 400 casualties and subsequently was too weakened to take part in the second stage of the Battle of Doiran two weeks later.

The next day, the 12th Hampshires returned to Deep Cut Ravine camp, collected and packed stores and equipment and moved back to a rear area. Arthur had survived this battle but another Great Rissington boy, Fred Vellender, had not. This action led to a stalemate in Salonika and the Germans referred to it as *'Europe's biggest internment camp'*.

Arthur was to spend the remainder of the war in Salonika. He was demobbed early in 1919 and he returned home to Great Rissington. He married Lily Archer in July that same year and they had three children; Sylvia, Joyce and Frank. Arthur died in 1977 aged 89. He can be seen in the demob photo 3rd left in the back row and in the parade photo 3rd row on the right.

Arnold Hathaway

7024 Private A Hathaway Coldstream Guards

ARNOLD HATHAWAY WAS born in Great Rissington in 1888 and was the son of John and Mary Hathaway. Arnold was one of nine children, including Harry, Wilfred, Gertrude, Lewis, Lizzie and Mildred. His father had been a farm worker but retired at the young age of 59 and his mother was a midwife in the village.

Arnold had moved to Birmingham by 1906, where he worked as a Billiard Marker. A Billiard Marker kept scores made by players and indicated them on a scoring board. On 14 November 1906, he enlisted into the 2nd Battalion, Coldstream Guards for seven years extended service with the colours. He completed this service on 14 September 1913 and was posted to army reserve. When war was declared on 4 August 1914, Arnold was mobilised at Windsor and posted overseas with the British Expeditionary Force (BEF).

War Diaries 2nd Battalion Coldstream Guards Regiment

12.08.1914
Battn entrained at Windsor in to trains at 3.10am & 5.15am for Southampton. Right half battn embarked on S.S. "Olympia" & left half on S.S. "Norvana" & sailed for Le Havre at 8pm & 7pm respectively

13.08.1914
Arrived Le Havre about noon. Disembarkation completed by 2.30. Marched to rest camp arriving 4.30. Weather very hot.

The battalion spent the next few days marching in very hot weather towards Belgium crossing the frontier on 23 August. In his book *'Heroes of the Great War'*, G A Leask says of the battalion;

> 'The men composing it presented such a smart appearance that the enthusiastic French people cheered the long line of khaki heroes as they marched through their towns and villages singing "Tipperary "on the way up to Mons.

23.08 1914
Marched at 3am. Still as advance guard to the brigade. Crossed the Belgium frontier at MALPAQUET at 4.30am. After a long, rather trying march reached HYON on the outskirts of MONS about 11am & after considerable halt, ordered to retire to QUEVY LE PETIT. On arrival here, battalion was moved up into the firing line at HARVENG about dusk & dug in.

Here Arnold's battalion rested before being thrown into the heat of battle. The troops held the line until ordered to retreat. This was the start of the retreat from Mons with over 70,000 troops under the command of Sir John French facing double the number of German soldiers.

War Diaries 2nd Battalion Coldstream Guards Regiment

24.08.1914
After a night without incident the battalion was ordered to vacate trenches at 3.30am & furnish rearguard to retirement of the Division, in conjunction with 3rd Battn Coldstream. A very hot, tiring day - retirement carried out without pressure from enemy but under considerable artillery fire. Reached LE FRESNE at 7.45pm & went into billets. (No casualties)

The retreat continued to Le Cateau and ended at the Marne after covering over 230 miles in eleven days. Here the British and French armies forced the Germans back to the river Aisne, saving Paris from being taken. After the Battle of the Aisne, Arnold moved to Flanders and fought in the First Battle of Ypres. It rained here for months turning the ground into a quagmire.

23.12.1914
Battalion marched at 8am N.E. from BETHUNE about 6 miles, waited about 3 hours and then with 2nd Bn Grenadier Guards took over a line of trenches from Sussex, Northamptons and K.R.R. just E. of LE TOURET. Trenches in very bad state. The men were standing in mud, slush and water over the tops of their boots, relief took all night.

24.12.1914
Trenches improved, another communication trench was started. Germans threw a few bombs and snipers caused a few casualties.

25.12.1914
Very cold and freezing hard. Snipers caused a few casualties, otherwise quiet. Defence arranged, 2 companies in trenches, 1 Coy in support and 1 Coy in Billet, relief taking place nightly.

At the end of January 1915, Arnold's battalion proceeded to take over the trenches at Cuinchy on the La Bassee road. Under continuous, heavy bursts of rifle fire and sniper firing all day, the battalion held the line.

War Diaries 2nd Battalion Coldstream Guards Regiment

01.02.1915
During the early morning the Germans threw a number of bombs into our advance trenches by the railway and forced the garrison to evacuate it, thus throwing the left half of the line and No 4 Company back to a Barricade of Sandbags. We counter attacked but were beaten off with rather heavy loss. Later in the morning our Heavy Artillery bombarded the position with, to the Germans, appalling results. The Field Artillery reached their remaining trenches and another counter attack was entirely successful, further round also being gained. In the two counter attacks the Irish Guards (No 4 Coy under Captain E B Greet) were invaluable assistance, both during the attacks and afterwards in holding and strengthening the defences of the position gained. Our casualties from 8pm 30.1.15 to 9pm 1.2.1915 were
Killed Officers 2 Capt Lord Northland and 2nd Lt J A Carter-Woods
Other ranks 20

Wounded
Other ranks 52

It was during this action on 1 February that Arnold was taken prisoner by the Germans and remained a Prisoner of War (POW) until the Armistice was signed on 11 November 1918. Most records of POW's are no longer in existence but when the war ended there were over 140,000 British POW's in Germany. According to Arnold's service records, he was shipped back to Hull on 11 December 1918 and was demobilised on 1 March 1919.

Wilfrid Hensley

Captain W H Hensley Somerset Light Infantry

WILFRID HENSLEY WAS born on 14 July 1894, in St Paul's parish, Warwick, the only son of the Reverend Henry Hensley and his wife Alice. In 1914, his father was the Rector at St John the Baptist's Church, Great Rissington.

Wilfrid attended Warwick School from 1904 to 1906. When his family moved to The Rectory at Great Rissington, he went to Dean Close School in Cheltenham until gaining a place at Emmanuel College, Cambridge University in 1913, where he studied Theology. He left before taking any examinations and enlisted, age 20, at Westminster, London on 15 September 1914.

Wilfrid was described on his attestation papers as 6ft tall, 12s 4lbs, with a *'good physical development, fair complexion, blue eyes and light brown hair'*.

Recruiting posters had appealed for 5000 men to enlist in the University and Public Schools Brigade, which would form the 18th to 21st Royal Fusiliers battalions. Wilfrid joined the 19th (Service) Battalion Royal Fusiliers, which formed part of the Second New Army, or K2. The four battalions were also called 1st, 2nd, 3rd and 4th Public Schools Battalions. The 19th R.F. were raised at Epsom, Surrey, on 11 September 1914.

Wilfrid did his training at Clipstone Camp near Mansfield. The camp was made up of wooden huts and Wilfrid arrived here in May 1915, along with five battalions of Royal Fusiliers. They helped set up the camp by establishing firing ranges and trenches. The camp could hold over 30,000 men, all digging trenches, practising rifle skills and marching about the country lanes.

On 14 December 1915, Wilfrid was at Tidworth preparing to leave for France. He left Tidworth Station at 4.30am, arriving at Folkestone at 8.40am and by 9.30am his battalion had embarked on a ship, which reached Calais, France at 12.55pm. From here the battalion marched to Boulogne and rested.

On the 16 December, Wilfrid moved by route march and train to Bethune where general work was carried out until the 20 December. The next day his battalion entered the frontline trenches at Windy Corner, Givenchy at 10am. They spent three days in the frontline affiliated to companies of a regular 1st Army Battalion who would show them the ropes. It was noted in the war diary;

War Diaries 19th (Service) Battalion Royal Fusiliers

The experience thus gained was extremely valuable and is likely to stand the Bn better than if it had been put into the trenches at once and without Bns & Coys from which to learn. For a newly arrived Bn the test was a pretty severe one on the whole as there were frequent moves and long marches to be carried out. The spirit of all ranks is admirable. Cas. 3 men wounded

After this baptism of fire, the battalion moved back to Hingette and Avellette on Christmas day, for 48 hours rest. By 29 February 1916, the battalion had vacated their billets and moved to Brickstacks trenches between Cambrin and Cuinchy, relieving the 20th Royal Fusiliers. Cuinchy was a small village midway between Ypres and the Somme. A major feature of the area were the brickstacks, which had been manufactured by a local brickworks. The trenches were over-run with rats at Cuinchy. Robert Graves spent time here and wrote about it in his book, *'Goodbye to all that'* (1929):

> 'Cuinchy bred rats. They came up from the canal, fed on the plentiful corpses, and multiplied exceedingly. While I stayed here with the Welsh, a new officer joined the company and, in token of welcome, was given a dugout containing a spring-bed. When he turned in that night, he heard a scuffling, shone his torch on the bed, and found two rats on his blanket tussling for the possession of a severed hand. This story circulated as a great joke.'

War Diaries 19th (Service) Battalion Royal Fusiliers

30.2.1916
Very busy overnight and during day. Very quiet in consequence. The trenches were in good condition but a considerable amount of work required to bring them into really fine fettle & withstand attack. Coincidently, an amount of wire footballs, sawstakes and concertina were put out. As far as could be ascertained the enemy had not touched their wire since the last month when we were in this subsection. The crater that was blown up on the 2nd Jan 1916 formed an enormous crater on the left of this subsection. The Eastern lip of the crater being about 5 yds behind our frontline. The dimensions of the crater were roughly 50 feet deep and about 50 yards across.

In March 1916, the battalion was moved to Racquinghem and lists of names of men recommended for a commission were sent to GHQ, which included Wilfrid. The Public Schools Battalions had many men who were considered to be officer material.

War Diaries 19th (Service) Battalion Royal Fusiliers

8.3.1916
The Bn was inspected by Brigadier General L.A.M.Stopford Commander General of GHQ Troops. The following were his remarks

"You could not have a nicer Battalion and I would not have missed seeing them. They are very steady in the ranks and extremely well turned out."

14.3.1916
The first batch of 50 men went to No 6 officers Cadet Battn Balliol College Oxford to undergo training with a view to taking up commissions.

Wilfrid joined No. 6 Cadet Battalion, Balliol College, Oxford on 15 March 1916. The training course, for officers, usually lasted four and a half months. The Officer Cadet Battalion held an establishment of 400 cadets at any one time. Over 73,000 men gained infantry commissions after being trained, with ever-increasing numbers coming from the ranks as the war went on. On 7 June 1916, Wilfred was discharged from the Royal Fusiliers on being granted a commission.

After his officer training, Wilfrid was appointed temporary Second Lieutenant and posted to 9th (2nd Reserve) Battalion Somerset Light Infantry (SLI), which he joined on 11 July 1916 in Swanage, Dorset. After a period of training, Wilfrid was transferred to the 6th SLI which was then in action in Arras, France. In April 1917 the weather conditions at Arras were cold, wet and snowy. The battle of Arras ran from the 9 of April through to the 16 May 1917 and was an attempt to break the deadlock in this sector. It was an effective attack but cost the British many men. The casualties totalled 84,000 British and the Germans 75,000.

War Diaries 6th Battalion Somerset Light Infantry

3.4.1917
First day of artillery preparations, the Battn moved to the caves where 3 Coy were accommodated. 1 Coy in our old British frontline.

4&5.4.1917
Rain, snowfall steadily during most of day, getting all the men soaking wet.

8.4.1917
All preparations made, bombs, rifle grenades, flares, very lights were issued

to the troops, also operation orders enclosed. The Battn moved to assembly trench and were in position at 12.25. Trench strength, 20 Officers, 560 Other Ranks. Zero was 5.30am. Our Brigade attacked at 7.30 with DLI & KOYLI, one of our Coys acting as moppers up to the KOYLI.

BEAURAINS
10.40am
Order arrived to proceed to NICE TRENCH & E + F lines. The movement as first completed at 11.30am, the hour passed for our advance of the WANCOURT. Coys advanced in artillery formation, B Coy leading C Coy, D Coy. A Coy was reforming & was coming on behind Battn HQ after mopping up.
11.30am
After some distance travelled Coys shook out into artillery formation, both flanks were completely in the air.
1.10am
A platoon of RB arrived on our left, showing somebody was there. About 80 prisoners were taken.
1.20am
We came under heavy enfilade machine gun fire from right flank and rear, owing to troops on our right not coming up. We therefore occupied a line about 600yds from our objectives and there consolidated.
4.00am
CLI were moved up to support us and form oppressive flank on our right.
6.15am
A warning order to prepare for an attack on the WANCOURT LINE received.
6.25am
Particulars received that barrage would lift at 6.45, 100yds every 2 minutes, finally lifting at 7pm off the WANCOURT LINE... the chances of our attacking successfully were small, however, our left flank advanced. DCLI were ordered to attack on our right, and the next division was 1200, (sic), in rear of us, the result being that our men were killed by German machine guns firing into their backs.
7.40am
Coys were ordered to consolidate their present position. Snowfall most of the night, bitingly cold, consolidation being very hard.

8.00am
Brigade ordered a composite Battn. to be formed with ourselves & DCLI, Lt Col. Bellew in command.

Wilfrid was wounded during this action on the 9 April and on the 11 April he was admitted to number 3 General Hospital at Le Treport, with a serious gunshot wound to his face. His father received a telegram, on the 14 April.

> "Regret to inform you second lieut. W H Hensley, 6 Somerset Light Infantry admitted 3 General Hospital Le Treport April eleventh with serious gunshot wound face. Will send further news when received"

Four days later, Wilfrid discharged himself and returned to the front. He could have taken the opportunity to get some home leave to recuperate but probably wanted to get back to his men.

Several telegrams and dispatches were exchanged between the hospital and the War Office registering surprise at his swift return. The War Office sent a telegram with the words;

> "If this officer was admitted to hospital seriously wounded on 11/4/17 he can hardly have been discharged 4 days later… could enquiry be made as to correctness of report."

On the 5 May, a reply was received confirming his discharge.

> "… confirms report discharged to Base Depot 15th April"

Wilfrid was promoted to Lieutenant on 26 July 1917 and again to Captain in December. He was then given leave to go home for 10 days and returned to The Rectory in Great Rissington. It would the last time his parents would see him.

According to the Rev. Hensley, Wilfrid was a promising officer but military service did not appeal to him and he was hoping to return to his studies after the war.

WILFRID HENSLEY

Wilfrid during his last home leave

This photograph was taken by his father during his last home leave in December 1917. Wilfrid is turned slightly away from the camera, possibly to mask the scar left from his facial wound. He left Great Rissington shortly afterwards and was soon back with the 6th SLI based at Amiens.

On the 21 March 1918, he was back in the frontline as the Germans launched Operation Michael. 6,600 guns pounded the British lines at 4.40a.m. The barrage was concentrated on British artillery and machine-gun positions and headquarters and was intended to knock out the British ability to counter attack. The weather was damp with a thick fog, which, together with the smoke from the bombardment, made visibility difficult. The 6th SLI were completely overwhelmed just after 9am, along with the 8th and 9th Kings Royal Rifle Corps.

During this attack the 6th SLI was reduced to a cadre and many men were killed or captured and taken prisoner of war. Wilfrid disappeared, probably blown up by a shell. His body was never found. The war diaries for this month were, not surprisingly, destroyed by shellfire during the battle and the following resumé was written afterwards.

War Diaries 6th Battalion Somerset Light Infantry

21.3.1917
At 4.30am the enemy opened an intense bombardment with all calibre shells, using a new kind of gas shell, the smell of which was not unpleasant, but had

the effect of sleeping gas. At 8.30am he finished gas shelling but continued with (open) shells it was very foggy, sentries posted at all points. All signal communication was cut by 4.00am. At 10.20am news was received that the enemy was in the frontline. Support Coy. Bn. HQ moved into strong points Egypt where fighting immediately commenced. 2 pigeons were dispatched and all papers burnt. The enemy at 10.30am were streaming down the ST QUENTIN road from both flanks and poured into LA FOZIE QUARRY. At 10.35am he was reported to be pushing towards BENAY and LENZY.

1 officer, 6 runners & 3 signallers commenced to fight their way to Bde. HQ with the news & to warn strong points. 1 officer reached Bde. 11.10am, 2 runners arriving 10 mins after. 1 signaller also got out successfully after which this party were attached to 9 Scottish Rifles in service trenches behind Bde. HQ. Estimated casualties, 20 officers, 540 other ranks actually in the frontline at the time of the attack.

The Reverend Hensley received a telegram informing him that his son was missing in action. On the 8 April, a letter was sent from a POW camp in Germany, from Captain Humphrey Burrington to his mother. The letter was noticed by the Postal Censor who brought it to the attention of the War Office. The Reverend Hensley received a letter from the War Office on 8 June stating,

> 'I am directed to inform you with regret that Captain H.S.Burrington, 6th Battalion, Somerset Light Infantry, a Prisoner of War in Germany in a letter which has been brought to the notice of the Secretary of the War Office by the Postal Censor has given the information that Captain W.H.Hensley, 6th Battalion, Somerset Light Infantry, who was reported as Missing 21st March 1918, was killed, but no further details are added.
> While it is feared that there is no reason to doubt correctness of this information, the question of its official acceptance as evidence of this Officer's death will form the subject of a further communication.

WILFRID HENSLEY

```
C O P Y.
S/7/54/9.                           RASTATT (Baden), 8th April 1918


My dearest Mother
         I hope that by this time you have got my post card saying that I am
all right. You must have been anxious not hearing from me for so long but
anyhow now you will know that I am safe for the rest of the war. I was
taken with a good many of the rest of the battalion on Marst 21st.
         *     *     *     *     *     *     *     *     *     *

         I expect Bellew will be anxious to know what happened to the
Battalion as he was on leave at the time. Will you tell Mrs Bellew that I
know of the following. Maj. Jerwood and Captain Hensley killed. Capts.
Hobhouse & Makins, Lieuts.Wilsie, Cotterell & Leivers wounded and
prisoners. Capt. Jellowlees, Lieuts. Hostler, Stafford, Twist, Burgess,
Drake, Thatcher, Scott, Estridge, Tucker & Boyce, Sergt. Major Giles,
Windsor and Flippen, Sergt. Gay prisoners. I donknow what happened to the
Adjutent or Gennery.

                         _____

Capt. Humphrey Sandford Burrington
      6th Somerset L.I.

     Comp. Block II
         Offiz. Gefg. Lag. Rastatt


Mrs Burrington
  Burnham on Sea
    Somerset
      England

                         _____
```

Captain Burrington's letter

Humphrey Burrington, who was a now prisoner of war in Germany stated that he had seen Wilfrid killed outright just before he had been captured. This letter was used as evidence of Wilfrid's death. Humphrey Burrington played cricket for Somerset before the war and afterwards became a solicitor in Barnstaple, Devon.

Pozieres Memorial, Somme, France

Wilfrid was killed at Moy St Quentin and is commemorated on the Pozieres Memorial on the Somme. The Memorial commemorates over 14,300 casualties who have no known grave and who died on the Somme from 21 March to 7 August 1918.

The following obituary for Wilfrid appeared in the Cheltenham and Gloucestershire Chronicle.

> **HENSLEY, WILFRID HENRY,** Capt., 6th (Service) Battn. Prince Albert's (Somerset Light Infantry), only *s.* of the Rev. Henry G. Hensley, of Great Rissington Rectory, co. Gloucester, Rector, by his wife, Alice Andrée ; *b.* Warwick, 14 July, 1894 ; educ. Warwick School ; Bath College ; Dean Close School, and Emmanuel College, Cambridge ; joined the Public Schools Battn. The Royal Fusiliers in Sept. 1914 ; served with the Expeditionary Force in France and Flanders from Nov. 1915 ; returned to England in March, 1916, and after a period of training at Oxford, was gazetted 2nd Lieut. 6th Battn. The Somerset Light Infantry ; promoted Lieut. July 1916, and Capt. Dec. 1917 ; was again wounded near Arras 9 April, 1917, and invalided home ; went back to France in Dec., and was killed in action north of Moy, near St. Quentin, 21 March, 1918 *unm.*

Wilfrid is also commemorated in Dean Close School's Chapel, Cheltenham and Emmanuel College at Cambridge University. In his Father's old parish church, St Paul's, Warwick, a stained glass window was commissioned to commemorate Wilfrid depicting the risen Christ.

WILFRID HENSLEY

TO THE GLORY OF GOD & IN LOVING MEMORY
OF CAPT WILFRID HENRY HENSLEY,
6TH SOMERSET REGT ONLY SON OF RT H.G. HENSLEY
SOMETIME VICAR OF THIS PARISH WHO
WAS KILLED IN ACTION NEAR MOY
ST QUENTIN FRANCE 21ST MARCH 1918
AGED 23 YEARS.

The Reverend and Mrs Hensley left Great Rissington in 1925 and moved to Ilmington, Nr Shipston on Stour. When they died in the mid 1940's their daughter Edith had Wilfrid's name added to the reverse of the headstone, where her own ashes would be buried in 1965.

Albert Higgins

Albert Higgins Headmaster, Great Rissington Board School

ALBERT HIGGINS WAS born in 1882 in Cheltenham. He was the son of a plasterer, John Higgins and his wife Emmeline. In 1901 the family lived in Hewlett Road, Cheltenham and Albert worked as a Pupil Teacher. Albert married Gertrude Caudle in 1908, who was also a teacher and they moved to Cirencester where they lived in Albion Cottage with their small son also called Albert.

On 15 June 1914, Albert took up the post of Headmaster at Great Rissington Board School and moved his family into the schoolhouse. Gertrude occasionally taught at the school during other teacher's absences.

Albert's occupation as a teacher was partly protected during the early years of the war and he was in no danger of being called up for war service unless he volunteered. On 12 May 1916 he went to Horfield Barracks in Bristol for a medical examination on the suggestion from the Education Board in Gloucester that Teachers should present themselves before their group was called up.

In 1916, men aged 18 to 41 could be called up for service unless they were married or in a reserved profession which could include teachers. This was later revised to include all men whether married or not.

On 19 May 1916, Albert presented the Recruiting Officer at Stow on the Wold with his exemption certificate, which had been issued from Gloucester. It stated that if he was certified fit for General Service he was not to be called up without reference to the Board of Education.

Albert continued running the school and teaching the children until 17 May 1918 when he was asked to present himself at Gloucester for a medical re-examination under the Ministry of National Service.

The National Service Act had been brought about owing to the large numbers of men needed at the front. It meant that Albert could no longer be exempt from war service on occupational grounds. From April 1918 the age of eligibility was also extended for men aged between 17 and 51.

On June 6 1918 Gloucester Education Committee issued letters stating that the Ministry of National Service *'could no longer grant extension of leave from Military Service'*. Albert received his call-up papers in July. He left Great Rissington and the school on 17 July 1918.

During his absence, his wife, Gertrude, took over running the school. Many women took over occupations previously held by men while they were away on active service. The School Attendance Officer, Fred Baber, was called up in 1915 and while away his wife Ada took his place.

It is not known which Regiment Albert joined but as he had previously presented himself at Horfield Barracks in Bristol it is likely to have been the Gloucestershire Regiment. I wasn't able to find a medal award for him suggesting he was not posted overseas. On 2 January 1919 Albert was demobbed and restarted his duties at the school as Headmaster on 6 January. He can be seen in the demob photo kneeling far left wearing his Silver War Badge.

Albert Higgins and the school children celebrating peace in 1919

Fred Howse

24921 Private W. Howse
Gloucestershire Regiment

WILFRED HOWSE WAS born in 1889 in Great Rissington and known as Fred. He was the son of John and Caroline Howse who later moved to Clapton Row, Bourton on the Water. He was one of several children and two of his brothers, Harry and Jack, served in the Rifle Brigade during the war.

Fred was lodging with Oliver Porter's family in 1911 and working as a Baker's Assistant for Harry Berry at The Bakehouse. In the spring of 1914, at the age of 25, Fred married Miriam Smith, a Stonemason's daughter from Great Rissington and they settled down to village life.

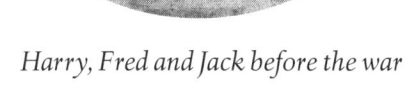

Harry, Fred and Jack before the war

In January 1915, Fred volunteered to serve with the Gloucestershire Regiment in the 8th Battalion and leaving Miriam at home he left to join his unit. After six months training at Clevedon Camp, Somerset. Fred left for France in July 1915, landing at Le Havre. Here Fred spent two months doing much the same as he had in England; route marches, bayonet fighting, trench digging, drill and taking a grenade course. On 24 September the battalion were issued further kit and the next day marched to Le Hamel, a reserve sector on the Somme, and bivouacked for the night.

Fred was to take part in an advance on enemy trenches but orders were given to stand down and the battalion remained in reserve. On the 29 September orders were once again received and Fred left his billet at 5.30pm and entered the trenches near Festubert.

War Diaries 8th Battalion Gloucestershire Regiment

29.9.1915
TRENCHES near FESTUBERT
Orders received re going into trenches. C.O. went round the subsection to be taken over in the morning and Company Commanders in the afternoon. Rained all day.

5.30pm. The Battalion left billets and marched to ESTAMINET CORNER where platoon guides of the 9th Cheshire Regt. took platoons into trenches. Trenches taken over from 9th Cheshires by 10.30pm. The trenches were in a very muddy condition owing to the rain which fell all the time.

When it rains on the Somme, the soil quickly turns into sticky mud that clings to everything. The trenches filled with water and mud caused the sides to collapse and fall in. In wet weather, men spent half their time shoring up the sides of the trenches and trying to keep their kit and rifles clean and mud free.

> "It's the end of 1916 winter and the conditions are almost unbelievable. We live in a world of Somme mud. We sleep in it, work in it, wade in it, and many of us die in it. We see it, feel it, eat it and curse it, but we can't escape it, not even by dying."
> Somme Mud, E Lynch (1920)

FRED HOWSE

War Diaries 8th Battalion Gloucestershire Regiment

30.9.1915
5.30am. Fine day. Spent most of day in cleaning up trenches. Everything quiet. A Coy employed parties during the night in burying dead men of the Welch Regt in front of the 1st line parapet. These men were killed in action of 25th Sept 1915.

1.10.1915
Enemy shelled the trenches between 12 noon and 4pm but no damage was done. Men were employed by day in making dugouts in Support Trench and clearing up GRENADIER COMMUNICATION TRENCH

2.10.1915
Hostile aeroplane flew from German lines as far as Support Trenches, but was driven back by ante aircraft fire. During morning, Germans were seen busy working at their trenches & our snipers had shots at them. Officers of 2nd Cheshires arrived in morning to take over trenches, and at 8pm the relief commenced and our last company files out about 11pm. Marched to bivouac at LE HAMEL arriving there by 1am.

The following year in January 1916, Fred was headed for Neuve Chapelle, a large village on the road to Bethune. There had been fighting here in 1914 when the Germans had taken the village. The British had re-taken it in March 1915 and Fred was now in frontline trenches just south of the village.

War Diaries 8th Battalion Gloucestershire Regiment

17.1.1916
11am to 2pm. Our field guns shelled the enemy's wire with a view to cutting lanes through it. During the bombardment our trench mortars, from direction of PLUM STREET fired several shots apparently with good effect, and the Germans were heard shouting, after some of the shots had fallen in their trenches. One shelter appears destroyed, as a piece of corrugated iron was seen sticking up over the parapet. While the trench mortars were firing, Coys fired several rifle grenades into the German trenches apparently with good effect.

The enemy retaliated with H.E. shrapnel on our front trenches without doing much damage. They also fired several H.E. shells about Battalion HQ on the RUE DU BOIS at 1pm and one shell burst direct on a dug out killing three men and wounding two others. The bodies of the dead were terribly mutilated.

The matter of fact way the diaries are written do not disguise how horrific the sights and sounds were on the battlefield and behind the lines. After his duties in the frontline trenches, Fred moved into reserve trenches and spent time here cleaning his equipment and receiving instruction on taking part in trench raids. By March he was back at the front in a trench called Signpost Lane. On the 14 March 1916, the Germans exploded a mine under a salient in the British line known as the Duck's Bill, owing to its shape.

War Diaries 8th Battalion Gloucestershire Regiment

14.3.1916
The battalion moved to billets at RILEZ BALLIEUL in relief of the 18th Battn. Royal Scots. The Battn. was under orders of the 106th Bde. The DUCKS BILL was blown up by enemy mine at 6.15am. Our Battn. Bombers were called upon to move to the trenches and hold the crater which is over 100ft in diameter. We were also called upon to relieve LAFONE & PUMP HOUSE KEEP. Our working parties were engaged all night on constructing a new breastwork in DUCKS BILL.

15.3.1916
The Battn moved to trenches in relief of 18th H.L.I. The trenches are the same as those held on the 3rd inst.

16.3.1916
At 7am we exploded a small mine under the SOUTHERN CRATER about 150° east of head of COLVIN STREET. Throughout the day the enemy were in action with trench mortars and rifle grenades.

17.3.1916
The enemy bombarded the DUCKS BILL CRATER with minenwerfer bombs. Between 30 and 40 were sent over doing considerable damage to work

done since the explosion of the mine. About midnight the enemy made a small bombing raid on the DUCKS BILL CRATER which was easily repulsed. The enemy continued to be very active with minenwerfer bombs and rifle grenades.

19.3.1916
A German of the 13th Bavarian Regiment came across to our lines and gave himself up. This is the first prisoner captured by this Regiment.

21.3.1916
At 10.45am enemy opened an intense bombardment on our frontline with shrapnel and H.E. The shells appeared to come from the direction of the BOIS DE BIEZ enfilading our line near MOATED GRANGE STREET. Considerable damage was done. The parapet was breached in several places and the supervision trench was in part destroyed. Many rifles and much equipment was buried. The bombardment lasted till noon. At 12.15 NEUVE CHAPPELLE was bombarded. Many of the shells were lachrymal and painful to the eyes.

Lachrymal was tear gas, which was used to frighten and confuse the enemy. Gas caused wide spread panic amongst the men and without protection it also caused temporary blindness. Those who experienced it would be incapacitated for some time. By March 1916, Fred would have been issued with a British Hypo helmet, for use during a gas attack. This was a simple canvas hood with transparent eyepieces and treated with chemicals. It was basic but worked, if put on quickly. When shells were found to contain gas, an alarm was sounded to the men to put on their masks. This alarm would merely be an old shell casing, which someone would ring by hitting it.

After the war, Fred returned home to Miriam. They later moved to Idbury, Oxfordshire, where Fred worked on a farm. They had two sons, Harry and Jack, named after his two brothers who had died in the war.

Fred's brothers, Harry and Jack, had both joined the Rifle Brigade. Harry was wounded in 1918 and was sent to a hospital on the south coast of England. He was given experimental treatment which involved using medicated wires to help heal wounds. He developed gangrene and was brought home to Moore Cottage hospital, Bourton on the Water, where he died two weeks later.

Jack was killed in action in Salonika on 15 April 1918 aged 23. His body was never found and he is commemorated on the Doiran Memorial. Both the brothers are also commemorated on Bourton on the Water war memorial.

Fred died on 3 June 1934 at the young age of 45. A gas attack he had been in during the war had contributed to his early death. The funeral service was held at St Michaels Church, Idbury and his coffin, which was draped in the Union Jack, was carried by Arthur Cyphus, Will Pill, Jack Pratley, Louis Webb, Harry Lane and Mervyn Berry who were all members of the Great Rissington branch of the British Legion. The Last Post was sounded at Fred's graveside by a former bugler of the Kings Royal Rifles.

Tom Hyatt

23696 Private T Hyatt Gloucestershire Regiment

THOMAS HYATT WAS born in 1898 at the Swan Inn where his father, Jimmy, was the publican. He was the youngest of five children including William, Mary, Lilly and James.

The Swan Inn

Tom attended Great Rissington Board school when Mr Demer was the headmaster. After he finished his schooling, in February 1912, he began working there as a Monitor. By 1913 he had become a Pupil Teacher.

At 13, pupils could stay on at school as probationers to help with the teaching of younger pupils. This was known as the Pupil-Teacher system. After two years as probationers, they would then spend another three years, learning to become a teacher before taking a final exam. If they passed, they would be paid to go to training college to become a qualified teacher.

Tom left the school on 26 July 1915 to join the 11th (Reserve) Battalion Gloucestershire Regiment. He was underage at 17 but by 5 December the same year he left for France and the front having been transferred to the 8th Glosters.

War Diary 8th Battalion Gloucestershire Regiment

Near Richebourg L'Avoue
19.12.1915
The Battalion went into the trenches today and relieved the 8th North Staffordshire Regt who took over our billets. Companies marched independently B & D into frontline trenches, C Coy into Reserve Trenches and A & 40 men of B into Reserve billets. Batt HQ on RUE DU BOIS near HAYSTACK POST. Relief completed by 9.30pm. Fine moonlight night. Patrols were sent out from frontline towards German lines during the night and our patrol reported enemy working on MOUND, FME. COUR D'AVOUE and trenches. Artillery were informed and fired on the objects. The Germans also had patrols out and about, 12 men strong.

The frontline trenches in this sector were full of mud and water, which clung to everything. It was at least two feet deep and in places waist deep. The weather was also bitterly cold and each company rotated every 24 four hours to avoid getting trench foot. The men were also issued with gumboots.

Trench foot was caused by standing for long periods of time in water or with wet feet. Feet became numb and all proper circulation ceased causing a dull ache to spread over the whole foot. As soon as men came out of the frontline trenches they had to dry their feet and put on dry socks and boots. In the early days of the war before Trench Foot was a recognised as dangerous, many men had their feet amputated after gangrene set in.

TOM HYATT

War Diary 8th Battalion Gloucestershire Regiment

20.12.1915
Enemy shelled our right section trenches near ROPE KEEP at 11am and 3pm but no damage was done. Our guns retaliated heavily. A patrol from D Coy on right went out at night and reported ground toward German trench very swampy.

21.12.1915
The 58th Brigade on our left, having arranged to loosen gas onto the German trenches, and then send six small columns of 2 officers and 20 men each to occupy the German Trenches. The Battalion was ordered to wear smoke helmets in the frontline and A Coy was moved from shelters in RUE DU BOIS to join the C Coy in Reserve Trench at 12.45am. At 1.30am orders were received cancelling the action owing to unfavourable wind. A Coy was therefore withdrawn.

3.15am Enemy fired 15 shrapnel shells on the Company HQ in our left section of the frontline trenches and wounded one man.

11am Our artillery bombarded MOULIN D'EAU works and parapet till dusk. A German machine gun played at intervals on PRINCES ROAD, the road from Battn HQ to the trenches. Our artillery fired three bursts of fire during the night.

6pm A Coy from RUE DU BOIS relieved D Coy in the right section frontline trenches. D Coy took up Reserve trenches from C Coy who moved up and relieved B Coy in the left section frontline trenches.

24.12.1915
Companies carried out kit inspection and 200 men were found for trench working parties under RE supervision

25.12.1915
Holy Communion 8.15am. Divine service in Company billets. Otherwise Christmas Day was not recognised except for an easy day.

Tom remained with the 8th Glosters throughout the war. He was badly wounded in July 1916 at the Battle of the Somme but recovered from his wounds and eventually rejoined his regiment.

Tom received the Victory and British War Medals and also the 1915 Star. It is not known what happened to him after the war or if he returned to teaching but he can be seen in the demob photo middle row, third left.

Harry Lane

29365 Private H Lane Worcestershire Regiment

HARRY LANE WAS born in 1890 in Great Rissington, the second son of Herbert and Mary Lane. His occupation in 1914 was a Threshing Machine Man. A threshing machine knocked out the grain from the ears of corn.

On 11 December 1915, Harry attested into the 14th Battalion (Pioneer) Worcestershire Regiment, at Stow on the Wold and went back home to await his call up papers. Special pioneer battalions were formed to meet the demand for skilled labour for the construction of trenches, gun emplacements and other field works during the long-drawn-out trench warfare in France. The pioneer battalions were not just labour units but were also fully equipped battalions fighting in the thick of battle.

Harry was mobilised on 9 February 1916 and was posted to Larkhill, near Salisbury for training. Training for pioneer battalions was more thorough than that of the ordinary battalions, because technical knowledge was needed as well as battle instruction and training. A lot of time was spent on Salisbury Plain digging trenches in practice for frontline duties.

Whilst at Larkhill, Harry got into trouble for overstaying a pass and was brought before the Commanding Officer of the battalion on a charge. The charge read:

> *'Overstaying pass from midnight 27.2.16 until 4.30pm 28.2.16, (16hrs 30mins). Forfeit 1 days pay'.* Harry was also confined to barracks (CB) for 3 days.

On the 20 June 1916 Harry moved to Southampton and embarked for France. When he arrived he marched five miles to Le Havre camp. From Le Havre he went by train to Bruay and marched to billets at Chamblain Chatelain, known as 'Charlie Chaplin' to the Tommies. His battalion then joined forces with the 63rd (Royal Naval) Division (RND) and came under their orders.

When the Royal Navy mobilised for war there were not enough ships to take all the sailors, so the Naval Division was formed including the 63rd RND. The Division had recently arrived in France from the Eastern Mediterranean and was in the process of taking over the trenches on Vimy Ridge. The 14th Worcesters marched to Bois de la Haie, three miles from the frontline and stayed in this area until for some months working on defensive positions where they were continually under fire.

On 12 November 1916, Harry's Battalion was back in the Somme frontline preparing for battle. The early morning was very misty and the 63rd Division was to attack at 5.45am. This obscured the men from the enemy, who were surprised and overwhelmed. The 14th Worcesters were soon hard at work consolidating the captured trenches and digging new works as the battle raged around them. By the morning of 14 November 1916, the German redoubt had fallen. Three tanks had been brought up from Auchonvillers and the enemy surrendered.

It is probable that Harry received his first wound during this action and was sent back to Blighty to recover. After a period of leave, he returned to France and found himself transferred to the 4th Battalion Worcesters, probably to bring this battalion up to full strength. Following the end of the Somme offensive, The Germans planned a major assault at Lys. The attack began on 9th April 1918, with an artillery bombardment lasting 36 hours and Harry was with the 4th Worcesters in the frontline. Captain J E Thornloe MC, the late Adjutant of 4th Worcesters recorded the following details.

War Diary 4th Battalion Worcesters April 10 to 15

9.4.1918

"*After a spell of approximately twenty days in the Ypres Salient, the Battn. was relieved and transported back to a camp some miles behind POPERINGHE. We had, however, only been there a few hours, when orders were received that we were to be ready to move off for an unknown destination in the morning, with the result that we only had about half a night's rest instead of as was hoped, a few days.*

10.4.1918

In the morning more definite orders were received and we rushed off in old London Omnibuses through BAILLEUL and down the ARMENTIERES ROAD, where we met a continual stream of refuges and some stragglers coming back. Some of the stragglers we collected and took away with us. A few miles from BAILLEUL, the Staff Captain met the convoy and stopped it proceeding any further in the direction of ARMENTIERES. We were informed that everybody was in full retreat and there was nothing between the advancing enemy other than a few stragglers. The only map of the area was in the possession of the Staff Captain. Col. Clarke who was in command of the convoy at the time. He immediately gave orders for three battalions, (4 Worcs 2 Hants and Monmouths), to disembark at once and sent the busses away. Being entirely dependent on that one map, he decided to seize the village of LA CRECHE and the station and railway embankment to the south of it. The enemy was advancing in considerable strength towards the village and along the railway. The 4th Worcs were soon heavily engaged, but managed to inflict severe loss on the enemy and reached all objectives. The fighting was severe at the station, which changed hands three times during the day but eventually remained in the possession of the 4th Worcs It was perhaps a curious incident and perhaps a fortunate one, that while the 4th Worcs were advancing to this attack, the remnants of 3rd Worcs were found to be retiring. Col. Clark took steps to have those men collected .... to take up position covering our right flank. The two battalions settled down side by side.

15.4.1918

"I cannot pass without paying a tribute to the fine spirit shown by all our men during this most trying period. It was a great feat to hold up the enemy for a period of six days, which undoubtedly gave time for re-organisation behind at very critical times. After our relief, we marched back to a well equipped Nissen Hut Camp, where the troops were given a really good hot meal and were soon between their blankets."

There were many casualties during this battle including Harry, who on 16 April 1918, was wounded for a second time, suffering a severe gunshot wound to the right arm. He was hospitalised at Eastleigh, Hampshire. When he returned to the front Harry had again been transferred, this time to the 1st Battalion, where he remained until he was demobilised on 13 February 1919.

He can be seen in the demob photo seated far right sporting his two wound stripes on his left arm. In 1922 he married Elsie Minchin and they had two children Mary and Richard. He died in 1934 aged just 44 and is buried in St John the Baptist's Churchyard Extension, Great Rissington.

Lol Lane

17641 Lance Sergeant H Lane
Gloucestershire Regiment

HORACE WAS BORN in 1890 at Little Rissington, the son of Michael and Elizabeth Lane. Michael Lane was a farmer in Little Rissington and he and Elizabeth had eight children, Eva, Blanche, Florence, Winifred, John, Horace, Cicely and May. Horace was always known as Lol by his family.

Lol enlisted at Stow on the Wold on the 23 September 1915 and joined the 8th Battalion Gloucestershire Regiment. His battalion was in the 57th Brigade, 19th (Western) Division, known as The Butterfly, which fought at the Somme, Ypres, Cambrai, Passchendaele and Saint Quentin. Much of Lol's time in France was spent in the thick of the fighting. He arrived in France just after the battle of Loos in September 1915 and by October he was getting his first taste of action in the frontline trenches.

War diaries 8th Battalion Gloucestershire Regiment

13.10.1915
TRENCHES IND IVY FARM CORNER to VINE STREET
10am Misty morning up to 10am. As soon as mist cleared at 10.35am a German Minenwerfer commenced enfilading our frontline trenches in the vicinity of BOARS HEAD from a point in the German trenches located opposite VINE and BOND Street. It fired regularly every three minutes and the fire lasted until 12.15pm. The holes made by the shells were of an

immense size and a large amount of damage was done to the parapet, which was breached in several spots, and communication stopped between A & B Coys. In the hour and a half 30 Minenwerfer burst. At 11am four H. E. shells burst near the junction of RUE DU BOIS and PALLMALL trench. Between 11.50am and 11.55am ten "pip squeaks" burst over the trenches on the left of our line. Our artillery gave us very little support during the bombardment. Casualties – A Coy, 1 killed, 1 missing (believed killed), 5 wounded, B Coy 1 killed, 9 wounded, D Coy 3 wounded. Several men were buried in dugouts and had to be dug out.

Lol with a group of Sergeants, 4th right, middle row

19.10.1915
A patrol fired through the mist on a German party working in front of parapet and dispersed them rapidly with loss. A German sniper's post was located. Enemy are continually working, building a strong redoubt in the German frontline. At 6.45pm our rapid fire and machine gun fire disposed of a working party of enemy. Enemy's fire of Maxims along top of parapet very active during night. One man of D Coy was killed whilst working on parapet at 7pm. 6.30pm our bombers from Boars Head observed a German looking over the parapet of their BOARS HEAD SALIENT. He wore a stiff green cap, like ours. As a bomb had just been thrown and exploded on the pest from whence he appeared, it is suspected that the salient has a bomb proof shelter at its end. Enemy snipers very active during the morning and broke three of

our periscopes. 12.30pm eight catapult bombs were fired on our trenches near BOARS HEAD. Six fell outside the parapet & exploded and one burst inside, but no damage done. 6pm One Coy of Gurkahs (8th) and 3 Coys Garhwal Rifles came in and relieved the Bn. Relief completed by 8pm

On 1 July 1916, the Battle of the Somme began, with the 8th Glosters forward in positions north of Albert, at 7.30am. On 3 July the battalion were in the attack on La Boiselle, and succeeded in capturing the village and the German trenches. The enemy counter attacked and in the end held the line running through the church, representing a British gain of only 100 yards. On the 6 July the battalion withdrew to Albert with 302 casualties. Albert was the main town used for billeting troops during the battle of the Somme. Here there were dressing stations, equipment dumps and other stores. The town's main church, the Basilica, had a golden statue of Mary holding a child Christ in her outstretched arms. This had been hit by a German shell in 1915 which left it at a precarious right angle. Superstitions grew surrounding the fate of the Virgin. The Germans said that the side which shot it down would lose the war The British said that when the statue fell, the war would soon end. Despite this It was secured by French engineers and later by British engineers with thick cable. When the Germans took Albert during their Spring Offensive in March 1918 and started using it as an observation post the Virgin's fate was sealed. It was targeted by British artillery and finally fell three months before the Armistice.

The golden statue on the Basilica today

War diaries 8th Battalion Gloucestershire Regiment

6.7.1916
Arrived at ALBERT – Battn. In billets near station – remainder of day passed in cleaning up and reorganising.

7.7.1916
Under Company arrangements – Baths were arranged for the Battalion during the day.

8.7.1916
Battn. was inspected by Major General Bridges and complimented on their recent achievements.

Lol took part in all the battles of the Somme offensive in 1916, the third battle of Ypres and the battle of Lys. The 8th Glosters were only second to the 1st battalion in the number of Battle Honours gained and the total men killed. In total the 19th Div suffered more than 39,000 casualties during the Great War.

Lol was demobilized on 18 March 1919 and married Eveline Hamblin later that year. By 1921 they had moved to Lower Farm, Great Rissington where they had two children, Arthur in 1921 and Elizabeth in 1923. Lol died in 1962 and is buried in St John the Baptist's Churchyard Extension, Great Rissington.

Percy Lewis

T/35666 Driver P Lewis Army Service Corps

PERCY LEWIS WAS born in Manor Park Road, East Ham, London in 1898. He was the second son of William and Harriet Lewis who came from Little Faringdon, Oxfordshire. At some point the family moved to Great Rissington where William became the publican at the Lamb Inn.

It is not known when Percy enlisted into the army but he served in the Army Service Corps (ASC). As with all things in the British Army the ASC was given a disparaging nickname and known as Ally Sloper's Cavalry after a comic strip character. Ally Sloper was a rent dodger and was always drunk and the cavalry reference was probably owed to the draught horses and mules the ASC used.

The ASC were one of the unsung heroes of the Western Front and were much undervalued. They transported everything the fighting troops needed at the frontlines, which included food, ammunition and equipment. They did essential work and although not directly involved in the trenches or attacks, they operated at munitions and supply dumps just behind the lines. They were not rotated between the front and rest areas as frontline battalions were because they were not fighting troops and night after night they ran the gauntlet of enemy artillery supplying and transporting the frontline troops. The Germans deliberately targeted the ASC to cause maximum disruption to the enemy frontline.

Percy was the driver of a Mule Transport team taking supplies to the front. His service papers have not survived, so it cannot be established which battle fronts he operated in. However, Percy's grandson, Steve, remembers his grandfather telling him stories of the war. Percy had reminisced about his time working with mules and disposing of some of the supplies he transported on the black market.

Around 800,000 horses and mules served the British Army on the Western Front. Over half of these animals died in the course of their duty. Percy told Steve of his terror when he first came under shell fire and of some of the terrible sights he had seen.

After the war, Percy returned to Great Rissington and married Liz Duester in 1921 and they had two children, John and Margery. For 18 years he was the landlord of the Lamb Inn. During the second world war, Percy became a member of the Home Guard and was also the village Air Raid Warden. If enemy aircraft were seen heading in the direction of Great Rissington, he had to walk around the village blowing a whistle to warn everyone to take shelter. When the danger had passed, he went round a second time to give the all clear.

In the early hours of 8 October 1943, a Wellington Bomber, flying on one engine, failed to make RAF Little Rissington runway and crashed into the garden of the pub killing all the crew except for the rear gunner, who Percy said had to be restrained from running back into the flames.

> "This brought most of the village out because they thought the invasion had started."

After Percy left the Lamb Inn, he moved to Windrush Camp where he ran a café. He died in 1973 and is buried in St Peter and St Paul's Churchyard in Northleach. Percy can be seen in the demob photo seated 2nd right.

Cecil Mace

204114 Private C J Mace Oxfordshire and Buckinghamshire Light Infantry

CECIL MACE WAS born in Great Rissington in 1894, the son of Thomas Mace and Mary (nee Garne), who lived at Manor Farm. Thomas Mace managed the farm for Mervyn Wingfield Esq. of Barrington Park. Manor Farm was one of five farms in Great Rissington and employed most of its labour from the village. Cecil would have had to take on a lot of the farm work when employees on the farm began being called up for the war. On the 1911 census he gave his occupation as *'hard working farmer's son'*.

Manor Farm

Cecil attested under the Derby Scheme at Stow on the Wold on 11 December 1915 at the age of 23. He then went home to continue working on his father's farm. As he was running part of the farm at this time, he applied for exemption from war service owing to his occupation.

Appeals tribunals were established to hear cases of men who thought they were in vital home service occupations, suffered ill health or conscientiously objected to war. An application for an Exemption Certificate could be made to a Local Tribunal who would decide if there were grounds for exemption from war duty. Cecil's claim form for exemption, dated 15 January 1916 was submitted to the local Tribunal, at Stow on the Wold and he gave the following reasons:

> *"As I manage all my business myself, it is impossible for it to be carried out in my absence. I have sold a quantity of hay to the war office, which I have to deliver, and it will be a great loss to me if I have to sacrifice my livestock and pay rent for land which I cannot farm.*
> *Cecil John Mace"*

Cecil was still living at Manor Farm at this time with his parents but was renting some land in his own name to farm on his own account. He also assisted his father at Manor Farm owing to the shortage of labour. Some trades were considered to be vital to the war economy and were called starred occupations.

As Cecil's occupation was not starred he came before the Stow tribunal again in February 1916 and applied for a further exemption on the following grounds;

> *"I have a farm, I keep a dairy, I milk and make butter, wean calves and have a quantity of poultry and attend to other live stock, do practically all the work myself. And in my spare time I act as foreman and go with machinery on a large farm of which my father is manager. I have been working on a farm since I left school in 1908. And I have been farming on my own account for the last four years."*

CECIL MACE

By October 1916, Thomas Mace was no longer the tenant at Manor Farm. He had taken over a farm at Fulbrook, Oxfordshire and Cecil was again assisting him in managing the business. As he had moved out of the area his particulars for exemption on the grounds of agriculture were passed from Gloucestershire to Oxfordshire and he now had to appeal to the Witney tribunal.

He wrote from here to the Territorial Depot at Oxford to complain:

> *"I am in receipt of your letter dated 15th January 1917, ordering me to join the colours on the 18th inst. & I write to ask if there has been some mistake, as I appealed to the Witney Tribunal for exemption on Dec 12/16 in accordance with the suggestion in your letter to me dated Dec 8th/16. This appeal is still pending & I have always understood that no man was called up until his appeal had been heard by the Tribunal. I also hold a letter under the signature of Lieut. Wood (Gloster) saying that as I was engaged in milk production, I should not be called up until Ap. 1st/17............ I farm 40 acres of land & have 4 cows, 19 other cattle, 3 horses, a quantity of pigs & poultry & as I have only one clear days notice you will readily see that it is quite impossible for me to realise my stock & clear up my affairs in so short a time, Will you kindly let me know if it will be correct for me to remain here until I know the decision of the Tribunal. Thanking you in anticipation, a reply per return.*
>
> *Yours respectfully*
> *Cecil Mace"*

Although it may seem that Cecil was simply trying to avoid going to war, he was probably worried about his father managing on his own with so little labour left. Most able men would have been called up so far on in the war and labour was getting scarce.

Despite Cecil's concerns about his land and livestock, he was duly called to the colours on 23 Feb 1917, and joined the 4th (Reserve) Battalion Oxfordshire and Buckinghamshire Light Infantry. He did his basic training at Hipswell Camp, Catterick and left for France on 16 June 1917.

In August 1917 Cecil was at Dambre Camp in the Ypres sector, Belgium.

War diaries 1/4th Battalion Oxfordshire and Buckinghamshire Regiment

04.08.1917
Brigade moved to DAMBRE CAMP, the battalion starting at 11.30am Order of march: H.Q. details, A, B, C, D. Route: to POPERINGHE, POPERINGHE – YPRES Rd, plank road N of VLAMERTINGHE and along ELVERDINGHE Rd, arrived 3.30pm. Found tents newly pitched and camp unimproved. Resting balance of day. A sunny day with occasional showers.

05.08.1917
*7.30pm
Early part of day quiet. Preparations to move into line for relief of 39th Div. Battalion moved of at 7.30pm. Order: H.Q, A, B, C, D; platoons at 5 minutes interval. Route:*

VLAMERTINGHE, plank road to SALVATION CORNER, road to left to Bridge 2A, trench board track to KITCHENERS WOOD. Took over frontline along STEENBEEK, from 6th Battalion CAMBRIDGESHIRE REG and 5th Bn ROYAL HIGHLANDERS.

Several casualties sustained going in. Killed: 2/Lt. R.H WHITE MC & REGTL SGT. MAJOR. R. LANE. The latter had been with battalion since coming out. Wounded: LT. W.H. ENOCH, adjutant.

06.08.1917
Relief reported completed at 1a.m. Dispositions: A & B left and right front companies, respectively; C & D in support. Former holding 2 Platoons at ADAMS FARM & 2 in CANOE TRENCH. Latter similarly distributed in THE BUND, a large concrete structure near

CECIL MACE

ALBERTA FARM, & CANOPUS TRENCHES. Bn H.Q. in CANOE TRENCH. 1/4th ROYAL BERKS in reserve in CANADIAN, CALF & CALIBAN TRENCHES. Battalion area shelled continuously during day, causing many casualties. 2/LT J. E BOYLE assumes adjutants duties. Clear bright day

Cecil was one of these casualties suffering gunshot wounds to his left knee and his testicles on 6 August 1917. He was sent back to Blighty to recover.

Cecil rejoined his battalion on 12 October 1917 to find he was being posted to Italy. On 24 November 1917, the battalion boarded a train in Savy station, which consisted of coaches for officers and closed trucks for the ranks. Cecil was to spend the next five days travelling to Italy passing through the old battlefields of the Somme on route. He was able to have baths and hot food at various stops on the journey. When the battalion reached Italy, the local people greeted the British troops with enthusiasm.

War diaries 1/4th Battalion Oxfordshire and Buckinghamshire Regiment

27.11.1917
Breakfast obtained at LES ARCS. Train left at 9.40am and travelled along the Riviera. Terrific reception by the populace especially and NICE and MONTE CARLO. There was great enthusiasm amongst the people who threw oranges on to the train. The weather was perfect and all ranks had a most memorable day. Food cigarettes, tea and postcards were showered on the men at all halting places

29.11.1917
On the last leg, the train halted continuously for periods of half an hour to two hours. At the halts the men played football and had great conversational struggles with the Italian soldiers.

Cecil was not to take part in any major action until the Battle of Asagio in June 1918. It was whilst fighting here that Cecil was wounded for a second time and had a short spell in hospital. He was sent home on 12 December 1918 and was demobbed in February 1919.

Cecil returned to his father's farm and took up his pre-war occupation. In 1929 he married Alice M Pratley in 1929, (not related to any other Pratleys in this book) and they had a daughter called Rosemary in 1931. Cecil died in 1980 while he was living in Buckinghamshire.

Fred Masters

1886 Pte F Masters Army Cyclist Corp

FREDERICK MASTERS WAS born in Great Rissington in 1893 and was the second son of William Masters and Clara (nee Taylor). Fred left school aged at 14 to work for the Bolters at Rissington Hill Farm, later moving to another farm in Little Barrington where he worked as a Wagoner, lodging with Richard Beauchamp and his family.

Sometime in 1912, Fred moved to Birmingham, where the wages were better, to take a job as a Carman, driving a horse drawn wagon that transported goods about the city. He was living in George Street West at the outbreak of war and attested into the Duke of Cornwall's Light Infantry at the Town Hall in Handsworth on 5 September 1914. At his medical, he was described as being 5 feet 6 ¾ inches tall with a chest measurement of 34 inches. He had a fresh complexion, grey eyes and dark brown hair. The Medical Officer also noted that Fred had a large mole on his left buttock.

Fred was given a rail pass and travelled to Bodmin in Cornwall two days later, where he spent 11 days training before being transferred to the 5th Battalion Royal Irish Fusiliers (Princess Victoria's) on 18 September 1914.

After three months, Fred was once again transferred on 1 December 1914, this time into the Army Cyclist Corps, 10th (Irish) Division's Cyclist Company moving to Basingstoke, Hampshire. Cyclists were used as a self-contained one-man fighting unit and as messengers. All Fred's kit was kept on his machine. During First World War operations, cyclists often had to abandon their cycles when the going got rough.

The Division received orders to proceed to the Dardanelles (Gallipoli) in June and Fred was posted overseas on 11 July 1915.

War Diaries 5th Battalion, The Royal Irish Fusiliers

11.7.1915 - Basingstoke
Marched out of camp at 01.00. Entrained by half battalions by 03.00am. Arrived at Devonport, 12.30pm and embarked on H.M.T. 'ANDANIA'.

The Andania was built by Cunard and requisitioned in 1914 as a troopship. She was a floating palace according to the men, with cabins rather than dormitories. Fred spent several weeks at sea calling in at Gibraltar, Valetta, Mudros. On the 5 August the battalion transferred to S.S. Osmanieh and landed at Suvla Bay in Gallipoli on 6 August.

Gallipoli was a major land and sea operation combining British, French, Australian and New Zealand forces in an attempt to invade Turkey. Conditions on Gallipoli were appalling. The rocky terrain and nearness of the enemy made it difficult to bury the dead. Flies and rats thrived in the heat and infested the trenches, which caused sickness and fever. Over two thirds of British casualties at Gallipoli were caused by illnesses such as dysentery and enteric fever.

As soon as Fred left the ship, he was in the thick of fighting.

FRED MASTERS

War Diaries 5th Battalion, The Royal Irish Fusiliers

7.8.1915
04.30 anchored in SUVLA BAY Action in progress on shore and two bombs dropped from aeroplane in close proximity to the ship. Proceeded to disembark in Motor Lighters in vicinity of LALA BABA, being subject to shrapnel en route, & on disembarkation ashore. On reforming Battalion near Lala Baba was ordered to attack Turk position on YILCHIN BERNU, moving by sand spit west of SALT LAKE. Thence ground N of Salt Lake and on to objective South, working in conjunction with the 6th R. Insq. Fus. on my right, and with the Infty Brigade on y left. We were very heavily shelled crossing the sandy spit W. of Salt Lake by high explosive and shrapnel which continued thro' out the day during the attack, rifle fire not being met with till entering ground N of the Lake and moving East across it towards enemy position. On moving to the Eastward over the above ground I found it very difficult to keep touch with the troops on my left as they apparently continued their advance in a N.E. direction over the spurs, & parallel to the crest line of KARAKOI DACH; and consequently in spite of my patrols & connecting files, I found my left flank exposed. As we got nearer to the position the sniping & rifle fire got heavier, the sniping being particularly prevalent on y left flank; now left open owing to the direction taken by the troops on my left. This condition became more pronounced as evening drew near & to prevent any further development, I threw my reserve slightly back on some slightly rising ground not far from Hill 50 at the same time notifying the firing line. By this I was able to check any attempt on my left flank such indeed as was made a little later on by the enemy from Hill 50. In few numbers Hill 53 (YILCHIN BERNU) was taken & my Battalion on it at about 19.00 that evening.
    Officers wounded, Capt. White. Casualties have yet to be ascertained

8.7.1915
Occupied Turk trenches. Some shelling. Sniping exceedingly prevalent and without intermission. Hill honeycombed with enemy trenches. Ordered to be ready to move to Hill 50 to relieved the S. Stafford Regt.

9.7.1915
At 02.30 moved to Hill 50 and relieved the S. Stafford Regt. Shortly after 04.00 heavy firing (rifle) commenced all round us; and it was very soon

apparent that an action of some importance was in progress. Our trenches were very shallow indeed & so narrow it was very difficult to move up & down them. Those hit had to remain a best they could. The men suffered severely from want of food & water and the delay in the supply of ammunition cause considerable anxiety. Casualties cannot yet be ascertained among the rank and file but I fear they are heavy.

Fred was living on the iron rations with which he had landed since no supplies were able to get to the battalion. He moved into support trenches on the 13 August and reinforcements arrived to make up the battalion strength. From the 15 August until the end of the month, Fred was engaged in heavy fighting and daily skirmishes against the Turks during which time five officers and 210 other ranks were killed, wounded or missing. He was wounded during this period and was admitted to a field hospital, on 31 August 1915, with shrapnel wounds to his left elbow and right thigh, and then transferred to No.14 Casualty Clearing Station (CCS) on 1 September 1915.

A CCS was a large medical facility, usually a tented camp, where a wounded man would be taken to from the battlefront. It dealt with any serious cases that were unfit for further travel. A typical CCS could hold as many as a thousand casualties at a time, and during a battle, could be overflowing. Serious operations, such as amputations, were carried out here.

By the 11 August, Fred was transported to the Citadel Hospital in Cairo, and then to the General Hospital, Alexandria, Egypt on 20 October. He was there for a few days before being sent back to England on the Hospital Ship, Asturias, on the 29 October and then sent to the 2nd Weston General Hospital at Manchester.

Fred never really recovered from his wounds and was discharged from the Army, having lost the use of his left arm. He was deemed medically unfit on 6 June 1916, with the following Medical Boards report.

"Cause of Discharge – Medically unfit G.S.W. left elbow"
(Gun Shot Wound)

"Originated Aug 31 1915 at Gallipoli. Flexion and extension of elbow only very slight. Pronation and supination practically none. Shoulder and muscle wasted, wrist and fingers very stiff."

Fred was awarded a pension from the Royal Hospital, Chelsea, of 18s 9d weekly on 13 November 1916. It came too late. Fred had died from the effects of his wounds in Selly Oak Infirmary, Birmingham, 26 September 1916. He was only 23 years old.

It was decided during World War One that all next of kin of soldiers who lost their lives as a result of the war would be presented with a memorial plaque and commemorative scroll from the King and country. The men referred to these plaques as The Dead Man's Penny.

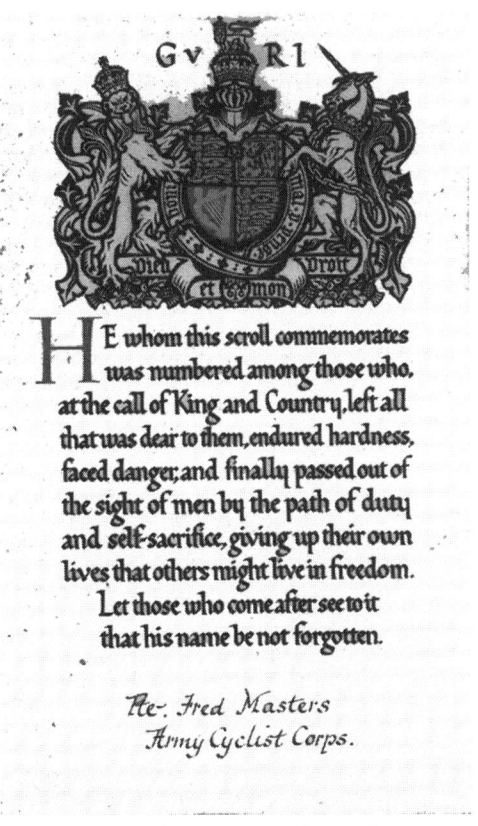

The scroll sent to Fred's mother

Fred is buried in St John the Baptist's Churchyard Extension in Great Rissington and his photo can be seen in the church.

Fred's headstone in the churchyard

The Mills Boys

FRANCIS JOHN BORN 1895 and William George born 1898, were the son's of Frank Mills and Hannah (nee Robinson). There were seven children in the family including Phyllis, Arthur, Herbert, Kathleen and Henry.

Frank senior worked for the Bolters at Rissington Hill farm where his daughters Helen and Mary were in service. When Frank left school at 13, he joined his father at Bolter's farm working as a Carter. William also worked here as a Farm Labourer as soon as he left school.

Frank Mills

13050 Private F J Mills Hampshire Regiment

FRANK JOINED UP with Arthur Cyphus and Fred Vellender attesting to the 12th Battalion Hampshire Regiment in 1915. His service papers have not survived but his battalion was posted overseas and he arrived in France in September 1915 for basic frontline training in Guignemicourt (west of Amiens). Frank's battalion was later selected for transfer to Salonika in November 1915 where he remained until the end of the war. For many who served in Macedonia this would be the last time they would see home for three years. Some would never come home.

Salonika is known as a forgotten front as it received so little attention. The first four months in 1916 were spent in digging trenches and laying barbed wire. So much wire was used, the area was known as the Birdcage. On 7 January 1916, German planes flew overhead and caused 18 casualties. Zeppelins came over during the next few months causing damage and fires, but HMS Agamemnon's 12 pounder guns eventually brought one down.

Frank, along with Fred and Arthur, spent his first few months in Salonika in bitterly cold weather, with heavy snows and freezing wind. The men had been kitted out in Mediterranean uniform, including shorts and pith helmets. It was a few weeks before they received warmer clothing more suitable to the bitter Macedonian winters.

On the home front, it was widely joked that the men in Salonika spent all their time digging gardens and growing tomatoes. But

Salonika only had ancient tracks used by goats and carts. The British Army spent their time building roads for men, munitions and supplies to use. The terrain was very mountainous and men had to work under constant shellfire from the enemy looking down on them.

The 12th Hampshires were in support of the 7th Wiltshires at Doiran in April 1916. It was during this battle that Fred Vellender went missing. The following is an extract is from the war diary of 7th Wiltshire battalion:

War Diaries 7th Battalion Wiltshire Regiment

25.4.1916
DOIRAN
On the night of 24th/25th April the Battalion attacked O1 and O2 trenches, 12th Hants attacked O3, 10th Devons, PETIT COURONNE. There was then strong T.M. fire and field gun fire on our frontline. The company went down the PATTY RAVINE in sections in file and formed up in line in the ravine on the N.W slope. The enemy put up a very heavy T.M barrage in the ravine during the whole of this time, which caused many casualties. The company crawled up the slope in line and having got to the top advanced to the wire. Gaps had been cut but it was impossible to get into the trenches owing to M.G fire on left of O1 and heavy rifle fire all along the line and enemy's bombers. Knife rests had been put up on the parapet behind the main wire and partly blocked the gaps. The Bulgars supports were seen coming down the CT. on left of O1 and the frontline was very strongly manned.

Our advance was held up and the company was forced to lie down in shell holes in front of the wire. The main party never got through the wire. A few got into the enemy trenches but were not seen again. By this time all the officers had become casualties and Sgt Townsend returned to our lines and reported the situation. He received orders from the company to withdraw and got what was left of them back to our lines, bringing what wounded he could with him. The enemy trenches were packed with bombers who had great advantage of position, as our men were unable to get through the wire. The company retried three times but on each occasion was brought to a standstill by the wire and owing to very severe casualties had no alternative but to withdraw to our lines.

All the officers with the exception of 2nd Lt Donne were either killed or wounded.

The attack on O3 failed. A portion of the attacking companies got into the trenches but were driven out by strong counter attack. Hants casualties about 450, Devons 500, D.C.L.I (who supported and reinforced Devons) about 150. During the next day the enemy artillery, after bombarding our lines at dawn was quiet. Stretcher parties led by M.O. went out at intervals during the day and brought wounded in. The trench mortar fired a few rounds otherwise the enemy did not interfere.

Frank spent his whole war service in Salonika and probably never had any home leave during this time. When he returned home in 1919, he went to live with his eldest sister, Helen and her husband in Windlesham, Surrey. They had a butchers shop and Frank worked as a butcher for them.

In 1921, he married Ethel May Vallens and they had three sons, Herbert, Francis and Ronald. Their son Frank served in the Ox and Bucks in World War Two and was killed by friendly fire in Holland in 1944. Frank can be seen in the demob photo standing 3rd right.

William Mills

23708 Private W G Mills
Gloucestershire Regiment

WILLIAM ATTESTED AT Bourton on the Water and joined the 8th Battalion Glosters in 1915, when he was just 17 years old. The 8th battalion was already home to several Great Rissington men and William probably had contact with a few pals from the village. It is interesting to note that William and his brother Frank joined the same two battalions as the Vellender boys who they had gone to school with.

William left for France sometime in October and was soon in the trenches at Neuve Chapelle. The British had lost 7000 men in the Battle of Neuve Chapelle earlier in the year, for a gain of just two miles, and were now holding the frontline against any enemy attack.

William spent time in the trenches before moving back behind the lines into billets. Here men were able to have a bath and get some rest. He spent February in reserve training and route marching. The weather was bitterly cold with heavy snow for most of the month. This was to be a fairly quiet period for William in the months leading up to the Battle of the Somme in July 1916.

On 7 May 1916, the battalion marched to Aire and boarded trains. The men were issued with blankets for the overnight journey and were instructed to close all doors at the sound of 'Advance' played on a bugle. The Commanding Officer noted in the war diary, that from this date, back badges were to be worn on field caps. The Gloucester Regiment had the unique honour of wearing a badge on the back of their caps for their gallantry in fighting back to back during the Battle of Alexandria in 1801.

The battalion spent the early part of June training and exercising for the coming Battle of the Somme.

War Diaries, 8th Battalion Gloucestershire Regiment

1.6.1916 St. RIQUER
Brigade training exercise the attack

5.6.1916
Brigade acted as skeleton enemy to the 58th Brigade manoeuvres.

On the 13 June, William attended a memorial service for Lord Kitchener, who had died when HMS Hampshire was torpedoed by a U-boat on 5 June. William continued practising for the attack and doing physical drill with the battalion right up to the end of June. The Battle of the Somme was to begin the following day and the 8th Glosters moved to the reserve lines on the 30 June.

War Diaries, 8th Battalion Gloucestershire Regiment

1.7.1916
7.30am Moved forward to Intermediate line N. of ALBERT
5pm Moved forward to valley near ALBERT POZIERES road

THE MILLS BOYS

10pm Moved forward to the TARA-USNA line rear of trenches and remained there the night.

2.7.1916
Battn in trenches TARA-USNA line all day

3.7.1916
1.30am Moved forward to attack St. Andrews trench
3.15am Attacked LA BOISSELLE & consolidated position - remained there all day & night. Officers killed Capt. H Cox, Capt F H Crooke, Capt W J Mason, 2nd Lt E G Evans, 2nd Lt F J Gadney, 2nd Lt J E H Ross

It was during the Battle of the Somme that William was wounded and sent back behind the lines to a Stationary Hospital near the coast. He was later sent back to England to continue his treatment. During the First World War a vast number of soldiers were wounded - including many with serious injuries and lung damage due to the use of poison gas.

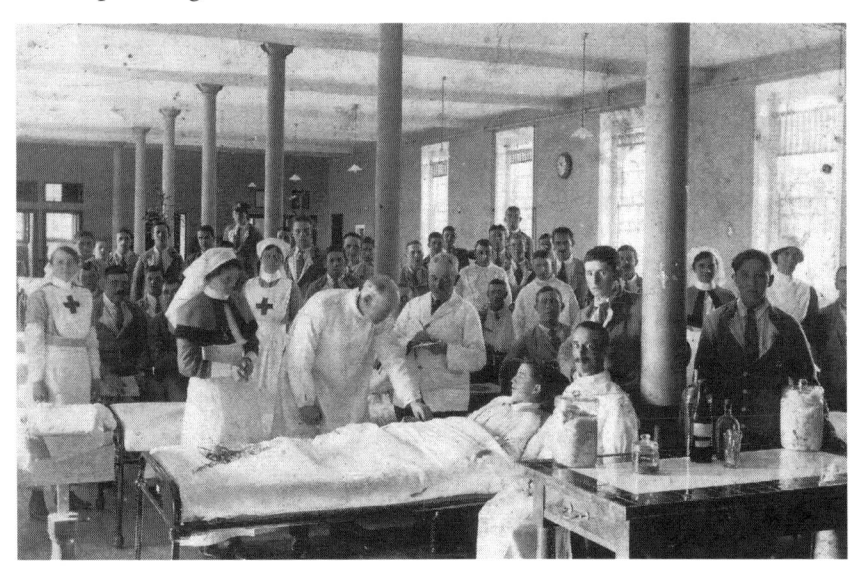

William can be seen in hospital, lying in the bed with a doctor and nurse in attendance. (The photo is probably posed for the camera). The walking patients are wearing their hospital blues, which they wore in place of their uniforms.

When William came home from the war he married Dorothy Davis, a Great Rissington girl. William and Dorothy moved to Heath Hill Farm at Wyck Rissington, where he worked on the land. When the farmer moved to Stoneleigh, near Stratford on Avon in Warwickshire he took William and Dorothy with him. They lived in a village called Ashow and had two sons, George and Harold. William died there in 1945. He can also be seen on the demob photo in the front row 3rd left.

Garnet Morris

242685 Lance Corporal G Morris Royal Warwickshire Regiment

GARNET MORRIS WAS born in Great Rissington in 1889, the third son of Richard and Anne Morris. He was one of nine children and attended the village school along with his brothers and sisters. In 1911, Garnet was living at home with his parents. His father worked as a Limestone Quarryman and Garnet was a Groom on one of the farms in the village.

Garnet was one of the first to volunteer enlisting at Bourton on the Water in August 1914, joining the 2nd Battalion Worcestershire Regiment. The 2nd Worcesters were part of the Regular Army that had formed the British Expeditionary Force, (BEF), and had left for France in August 1914. In September and October 1914, the battalion received several reinforcements of men, to replace those lost at Mons, Marne, Aisne and the first Battle of Ypres. After a period of training, Garnet was posted overseas to bring the battalion up to strength.

Garnet's first taste of action would be during the Battle of Loos between 25 September and 19 October 1915. It was referred to as the Big Push and a huge bombardment of the German trenches started on the 21 September and dummy attacks by the British were undertaken to persuade the enemy to man their trenches. These included using dummy troops, bayonets being shown over the parapet and men shouting. On the 24 September the British Army used poison gas for the first time but it was not a success because the wind blew the gas back over the British lines. The gas was released at 5.50am and Garnet went over the top at 6.30am. The battle ended on 28 September with the British suffering 50,000 casualties while the Germans lost about 25,000 men.

By January 1916, Garnet had moved to Bethune, a mining area in Northern France, and into trenches at Givenchy. The weather had been terrible and the trenches were in a poor condition.

War Diaries 2nd Battalion Worcestershire Regiment

1.1.1916
The trenches were in a bad state. ORCHARD REDOUBT knee deep in mud.

2.1.1916
A quiet night. At 9.30am Enemy commenced sending Minenwerfers into our right front platoon and the mine head on CANAL BANK and damaged it badly burying 3 miners and killing a Sergeant and a man of ours and wounding 3 men.

Mining activities on the Western Front were undertaken by both sides during the war. Once a mine was blown, both sides would rush to take charge of the crater caused by the explosion.

War Diaries 2nd Battalion Worcestershire Regiment

3.1.1916
Intermittent shelling by guns of light calibre during the whole night. No damage was done. Quiet all along our frontline. The whole section was heavily shelled from 3pm to 4pm, which died down and finally ceased about

4.15pm. Working parties were employed all night on right frontline BAKER STREET and CHEYNE WALK repairing damage done by shelling yesterday. Listening posts were sent out during night close up to the German wire. No sounds of enemy were heard. Their flares seemed to be sent up from their 3rd line. About 6.30pm our guard on PONT FIXE BRIDGE reported a lamp signalling from direction of enemy's trenches south of canal and twice read 'JOHN BULL'.

A listening post, also known as a Sap Head, was a shallow, narrow position about 30yds in advance of the frontline, in No Mans Land. They were used to keep an eye on the enemy and to gather information.

Garnet spent the next few months in Bethune, rotating between the frontline and reserve trenches. In mid July, the battalion moved to bivouacs in Fricourt in preparation for an attack on High Wood, in the Battle of Bazentin Ridge. Over a period of two months, High Wood was held by the enemy, despite repeated attacks. It is estimated that the remains of over 8000 soldiers from both sides still lie in the wood today.

The Battle of Bazentin Ridge was part of the second phase of the Somme Offensive. After a short artillery bombardment, the men went over the top and took the Bazentin Le Petit and Bazentin Le Grand Woods in a few hours. The Germans seemed to have abandoned High Wood and the cavalry were used initially to break through with the infantry to follow. The delay in using the infantry allowed the Germans to move back into the wood and man their machine gun posts. Garnet was in the attack on the German Switch Line Trench and despite repeated attempts and devastating losses, the attack was unsuccessful.

War Diaries 2nd Battalion Worcestershire Regiment

14.7.1916
The battalion left FRICOURT about 3pm and marched through MAMETZ village up to MAMETZ WOOD. The battalion dug in near FLATIRON COPSE under a steep bank. There was a good deal of shelling went on during the night and the Huns sent over a number of Lachrymatory shells. (Tear Gas)

15.7.1916
The Bn marched off in the mist about 5am and passed BAZENTIN-Le-GRAND WOOD and finally formed up in reserve position between the BAZENTIN Road and HIGH WOOD. The 100th Infantry Brigade was ordered to attack. The Glasgow Highlanders and 1st Queens (RWS) Regt were in the frontline on the left and right respectively. The 16th K.R.R. were in support and the 2nd Worcesters were in reserve. The 9th H.L.I. were held up by fire from HIGH WOOD and were unable to clear the wood.

The 2nd Worcesters were sent in to help and advanced across the open to the original jumping off trench of the 9th Highland Light Infantry and then tried to attack the Switch Line, but the attack was held up by German machine-gun fire from High Wood. Garnet and the 2nd Worcesters were eventually relieved at 3am on the 16th July and returned to their bivouacs behind the lines.

The Somme offensive ended in November 1916 and the following spring between 12 March and 5 April 1917 the Germans retreated to the Siegfried Line. This was a formidable defence system they had built during 1916 and 1917. The concrete and steel fortifications extended from the Swiss frontier to Luxembourg and consisted of deep and wide trenches, thick belts of barbed wire, concrete machine-gun positions, steel and concrete bunkers, tunnels and command posts. The whole area that they abandoned was completely destroyed so as not to leave anything of use in their enemy's hands. Villages were reduced to rubble, trees felled, wells poisoned and booby-traps laid.

After the Battle of the Somme Garnet was transferred to the 1/6th Royal Warwickshire Regiment, possibly after a period of leave. Men were frequently transferred on their return to the Base Camp in France, to make up losses in other battalions.

War Diaries 1/6th Battalion Royal Warwickshire Regiment

1.4.1917
The Bttn. took part in an attack by Infantry Brigade on EPEHY and POZIERESs. The Bttn. attacked and was supported by 1/5th Royal Warwickshire Regt. - B, C and D Coys. had A Coy. in reserve. Attack

commenced at dawn. The whole objective was secured by 6.40am. Casualties - 2/Lt. R B W Gosse died of wounds. Lt G H L Eastbrook, wounded. Captured one field and machine gun.

2.4.1917
Held new outpost line in front of EPEHY - Casualties, 2/Lt S E Bowden wounded. OR's, 1 killed, 1 died of wounds, 2 wounded. Relieved at dusk by 1/5th R. Warks Regt. D.C.M. granted to No; 240276 Pt. Richmond DC.

3.4.1917
In support of HQ and B & C Coys. in SAULCOURT WOOD.

Garnet and the battalion moved to reserve trenches at Templeux la Fosse for a short spell, where they repaired the roads before returning to frontline duties. On the 14 April, the battalion moved to the frontline trenches at Pozieres.

War Diaries 1/6th Battalion Royal Warwickshire Regiment

14.4.1917
Relieved 5th Lancashire Fusiliers on left Bttn front. A Coy. Dug in four posts.

Garnet took part in an attack on Pigeon Ravine on the night of the 16 April. The night was pitch black with wind and driving sleet.

War Diaries 1/6th Battalion Royal Warwickshire Regiment

16.4.1917
Carried out a night attack with 5th Royal Warks on right. Assault timed for 10pm. Terrible weather conditions. Objective gained on half the front. Capt. J N G Stafford and 2/Lt J Harrison killed. Casualties - OR, 10 killed, 32 wounded, 2 missing, captured 1 machine gun

Night attacks on enemy trenches were usually frightening for both sides, involving hand-to-hand fighting in cramped spaces in the dark. Garnet was killed in action on the 16 April 1917 but his body was never found.

He is commemorated on the Thiepval Memorial on the Somme. The introduction to the Thiepval register, published in the 1930s, says of those commemorated here

> "A few will be found and identified as the woods are cleared, or when the remaining tracts of devastated land are brought under the plough. Many more are already buried in the larger British cemeteries of the Somme, but as unidentified. To the great majority this memorial stands for grave and headstone, and this register for as proud a record as that for any grave."

Garnet's name carved into the Thiepval Memorial

Teddy Parker

212397 Driver E T Parker, Royal Field Artillery

EDMUND PARKER WAS born in 1894 in Aldsworth. He was the eldest son of William and Julia Parker who later moved to Great Rissington. Edmond was known as Teddy and had three older sisters, Margaret, Jane and Agnes. William worked as a shepherd and when Teddy left school he went to work with his father on Manor Farm.

Teddy's service papers have not survived so I have been unable to pinpoint any action he may have been involved in. The Royal Field Artillery was responsible for the medium calibre guns and howitzers. They were deployed close to the frontline and could be moved fairly quickly. A Battery at full strength would consist of 198 men. A typical Field Gun Battery would include, a Major and Captain, 3 2/Lieutenants in charge of two gun sections. The Battery also included a Sergeant Major, a Farrier, Shoeing Smiths, Saddlers, Wheelers, Gunners and Drivers.

Drivers rode the horses that pulled the guns but were also trained as gunners so they could replace any men knocked out of action. Batteries were rarely at full strength, with equipment lost or destroyed. Guns were sometimes abandoned in difficult situations. Men would usually try to destroy their guns first rather than let them fall into enemy hands.

Teddy was wounded in the chest on 03 January 1917 and spent time in a hospital in Torquay to recover before being invalided out of the army. He married his first wife Alice Beasley in 1918 and lived at Barrington Bushes where he worked for Barrington Park Estate.

Alice died in the early 1940's and Teddy then married Emily Vellender in 1944, sister to Fred and Jack. They continued to live at the Bushes, later moving to North Lodge where Teddy worked for Rissington Hill Farm. When Teddy took a job working on the roads, they moved to Blue Close Cottage in Rectory Lane. He died in 1974 aged 80 years old.

It is possible that Teddy is the man far left, back row on the demob photo. He is certainly wearing an Artillery cap badge on his lapel and he does have similar features.

The Pill Boys

WILLIAM, HENRY AND Albert were the sons of Edwin Pill and Mary (nee Brunsden). William (1883) and Albert (1898) were born in Holwell and Henry (1887) in Signet, two small parishes near Burford, Oxfordshire. The family later moved to Great Rissington. The boys were known as Will, Harry and Bert.

Will Pill

31233 Private W Pill Gloucestershire Regiment

In 1905, Will married Emily Bartlett and they took a cottage in Great Rissington where he worked as a road contractor. At the start of the war in 1914 they had five children all under nine years old.

Will enlisted into the 8th battalion Glosters sometime in 1915. After his training he embarked for France and arrived at Le Havre in October 1915. On 1 July 1916, the Battle of the Somme began, with the 8th Glosters forward in positions north of Albert, at 7.30am. On 3 July the battalion were in the attack on La Boiselle, and succeeded in capturing the village and the German trenches. The enemy counter attacked and in the end held the line running through the church, representing a British gain of only 100 yards.

Will served in the same battalion as Oliver Porter and John Vellender, who were both killed on the Somme. He took part in all the battles of the Somme offensive in 1916, the third battle of Ypres and the battle of Lys.

In October 1915, the 8th Glosters were in the frontline trenches known as the 'Boars Head'. The Boars Head was once part of the German support line, which became the new British frontline and was named because of its shape resembling a boar's head.

'TIL THE BOYS COME HOME

War Diaries 8th Battalion Gloucestershire Regiment

14.10.1915
From 3.30pm to 4pm our artillery fired shells (HE) on FME DU BOIS. All quiet in the afternoon and evening. During the bombardment our casualties, chiefly due to minenwerfers were 2 killed, 10 missing, 8 wounded. Several men were buried in dugouts and had to be dug out. During the night Coy's worked continuously to repair damage.

15.10.1915
7.30am
A German walking along his parapet thinking the mist sufficient cover was "dropped" by one of our snipers.

8.15am
A patrol in the mist got within 100yds of a German party working in front of their parapet. The patrol opened rapid fire and three Germans fell and more were hit. Enemy working hard all day at the spot from whence the minenwerfer was seen to be firing yesterday.

12.45am
Hostile "pipsqueaks" burst near front parapet, no damage done. Rifle grenades were sent near trenches by BOARS HEAD during the night doing no damage. Work by day and night chiefly on front parapet, which was breached in several places by the minenwerfer on the 14th

16.10.1915
7am
Two of our machine guns fired from trenches on German working parties in the mist. The mist prevented our seeing the result.

2.40pm
Our artillery dispersed a German party working in their support trenches. Our snipers were active. During the night, seven mysterious missiles fell behind RANGERS TRENCH but they failed to explode and there is no trace of them.

THE PILL BOYS

17.10.1915
Misty morning and quiet all day. Enemy hard at work on their defences. Our snipers active. More missiles were sent over during the evening from a gun, the report being slightly louder than a rifle. Enemy fired rifle grenade on trenches near BOARS HEAD during the night to which we vigorously retaliated.

18.10.15
11am
A German in dark green uniform was spotted on German parapet for a second or so. Shrapnel and H.E.shells fell about trenches. One shrapnel burst near EMBANKMENT TRENCH and at the same time a catapult bomb from which there was 5 casualties and EMBANKMENT TRENCH blocked up. Our guns vigorously retaliated and enemy fire ceased. 3pm Our "heavies" bombarded the spot from which the minenwerfer fired on the 14h and made very good shooting. 4pm Our snipers fired on a German working party and dropped three men and a fourth was dragged over the parapet. 9pm A trench mortar (minenwerfer) bomb explode between the two front trenches, no damage

19.10.1915
7am A patrol fired through the mist on a German party working on part of the parapet and dispersed them rapidly with loss. A German snipers post was located. Enemy is continually working on a strong redoubt being made in the German frontline. At 6.45pm our rapid fire and machine gun fire dispersed a working party of enemy. Enemy's fire of maxims along the top of parapet very active during the night. One man killed whilst working on parapet at 7pm. 6.30am Our bombers from BOARS HEAD observed a German looking over parapet of BOARS HEAD salient. He wore a stiff green cap like ours. As a bomb had just been thrown and exploded on the part from whence he appeared. It is suspected that the salient has a bombproof shelter at the end of it. Enemy's snipers very active during the morning and broke three of our box periscopes.

12.20pm
Light catapult bombs fired across trenches near BOARS HEAD. 6 fell outside the parapet and exploded and 2 burst inside, but no damage done. Catapult was located.

6pm
One company of 8th Ghurkhas and 3 companies Ghurkha Rifles came in and relieved the Battalion. Relief completed by 3pm.

Will remained in the 8th Battalion throughout the war and was demobilised early in 1919. He returned to Great Rissington and to Emily and the children. He died in 1948 and is buried in St John the Baptist's Churchyard Extension. Will's son Bill was a well known character in the village. Will can be seen in the demob photo standing 2nd right and also in the parade photo 2nd row on the left.

Harry Pill

31425 Private H Pill Hampshire Regiment

HARRY PILL SERVED in the Hampshire Regiment, transport section. Transport sections provided frontline trenches with stores and ammunition for all weapons. They also transported food and limber. Harry would have helped take care of the horses used by the Commanding Officer and Company Commanders as well as the battalion horses. Horses played a vital role in the war. They were so heavily relied on that over 8 million died on all sides fighting in the war.

Harry suffered from shell shock caused by the constant fear of being killed and the continual noise of the guns. Between 1914 and 1918, 80,000 men were acknowledged as suffering from shellshock. In the beginning, men were suspected of being malingerers and sent back to the front. Some committed suicide and others simply broke down. Men who deserted under the pressure were court martialed and could end up being shot at dawn.

Shellshock was, at first, thought to be caused by the men being constantly exposed to explosions and shellfire. There didn't seem to be any physical symptoms and doctors were unable to diagnose the problem. The men were often treated harshly and would be put into solitary confinement. As the war progressed and the condition became better understood, men were sent home to recover. However, the effects of shellshock could be felt for years after the war. Some men never recovered.

Harry spent some time in a hospital in France before being sent to a hospital in Weymouth to recover. (Possibly Princess Christian Hospital, Weymouth). He never returned to the front.

His Granddaughter, Jean, says 'he was a really gentle man, who was badly affected by the war for the rest of his life.' Harry married Ellen Rouse in 1920 and they had a daughter, Elsie in 1922. He died in 1962 and is buried in St John the Baptist's Churchyard in Fifield, Nr Burford.

Bert Pill

21194 Sgt A Pill Gloucestershire Regiment

BERT WAS HARRY and Will's younger brother. It is known that he served in the 8th Battalion Gloucestershire Regiment and I have been able to establish his Regimental number from the National Archives and also his rank from the demob photo. However, as Bert's service papers did not survive, and with no family stories to build on, I have been unable to write any detail of Bert's war duties. Bert served in the same battalion as several men from Great Rissington so may have been involved in some of the actions in which they fought. His great niece, Jean, told me he was gassed during the war and suffered the effects for many years. The following extract is from an anonymous British eyewitness account of a German gas attack.

> *"Utterly unprepared for what was to come, the [French] divisions gazed for a short while spellbound at the strange phenomenon they saw coming slowly toward them.*
>
> *Like some liquid the heavy-coloured vapour poured relentlessly into the trenches, filled them, and passed on.*
>
> *For a few seconds nothing happened; the sweet-smelling stuff merely tickled their nostrils; they failed to realize the danger. Then, with inconceivable rapidity, the gas worked, and blind panic spread.*
>
> *Hundreds, after a dreadful fight for air, became unconscious and died where they lay - a death of hideous torture, with the*

frothing bubbles gurgling in their throats and the foul liquid welling up in their lungs. With blackened faces and twisted limbs one by one they drowned - only that which drowned them came from inside and not from out.

Anon"

Bert died in 1979 in Shropshire but can be seen in the demob photo standing third from right.

Oliver Porter

13647 Pte O J Porter Gloucestershire Regiment

OLIVER JOHN PORTER was born in Great Rissington in 1895, the son of William and Fanny Porter. Oliver's father had been a shoemaker but before the war was working on one of the five farms in Rissington as a labourer. When the Great War broke out, Oliver was working as a plumber's assistant but was keen to volunteer. He enlisted at Bourton on the Water, 18 May 1915, joining the 8th (Service) Battalion Gloucestershire Regiment.

The 8th Battalion was in the 19th (Western) Division, which had been formed on Salisbury Plain but when Oliver enlisted, the Division had moved to billets in Weston and Clevedon. Oliver trained as a battalion machine gunner. In June 1915, King George V inspected the 19th Division just before it left for France.

Oliver landed in Le Havre on 18th July 1915 and on 28th August the 8th Glosters moved into the frontline. Two Companies would be in the frontline trench with the other two in reserve trenches. They exchanged places every four days. Time here was spent repairing trenches, putting out wire entanglements and sending out patrols into no man's land.

As a battalion machine gunner, Oliver would be watching for German patrols, raids and attacks and firing at any movement from the other side. The trenches in this sector were quite close together and the Germans would often be heard moving about and talking to one another.

War Diaries 8th Battalion Gloucestershire Regiment

1.9.1915
Our artillery during the day fired several shells on enemy's positions, enemy's reply being feeble. 5.30am, Enemy's rifle grenades were fired onto C Companies 1st line trench, but no damage was done. 10.00am, C Company fired on party of Germans with machine gun seen in old German trench in front of FERME COUR D'AVOUE. Result not known. 10.30am, A & C Company working party again had to go back to their 1st line trenches from working in front, owing to enemy's machine gun & artillery fire. 10.30am, Enemy's Machine gun fire swept along parapet of Reserve Trenches and two men of B Company working in front were wounded. 11am, Corporal Cox "C" Company shot three Germans who were crawling about near old German trench. Two rolled over & the third crawled away wounded. The same N.C.O. fired at a German seen by listening post at 5.30pm. After the shot, the man ran away with his clothes in flames. 2.30pm, our guns shelled FERME COUR D'AVOUE at Midday the Germans shelled house along RUE DU BOIS just behind our Reserve Trenches. 7pm, B & D Companies relieved A & C Companies in 1st line & support trenches and A & C took up positions in Reserve Trenches. B Coy also took over WATER KEEP and C Company FALLEN TREE KEEP.

Patrols of officers and men were sent out each night to creep up to the enemy trenches in the hopes of capturing a prisoner or finding out information.

War Diaries 8th Battalion Gloucestershire Regiment

5.9.1915
11pm, Lieut Masa, 2/Lt Fitzgerald & one man of D Coy patrolled old German communication trench 100 yards in front of 1st line trenches & found several dead Germans. They brought back valuable information in the shape of articles of equipment and newspapers. At 8pm a signaller read a German signalling lamp and made out the words, "Kitchener. Transport. Halt. Officers."

6.9.1915
7pm, A Company relieved B Company in the 1st line trenches and support and at 8.30pm C Company relieved D Company taking up Reserve Trenches.

7..9.1915
10.30am, A L.G.V. German Biplane flew over trenches from west to east.11pm, Capt Fry & Lieut Hastings accidentally wounded in revolver accident.

10.9.1915
Capt Byers & Lt Fitzgerald & 1 man D Coy patrolled towards German lines in the morning. Brought back useful report and various articles of German equipment. A & B Coy Officers patrol reported working party between FERME DU BOIS & FERME COUR D'AVOUE at 5.30 pm & reported Germans advancing their line of trench between three farms. Rapid fire on working party at 7pm resulted. At 4pm a German biplane was hit by our anti aircraft & seen to fall near BOIS DU BIEZ. At 5.30pm Germans fired machine gun on trenches in advance of their trench line.

11.9.1915
Our working parties in front of 1st line trenches were fired on by "whiz bangs" machine gun & rifle fire but suffered no casualties, otherwise quiet day.

12.9.1915
5am, Germans from near FERME COUR D'AVOUE were heard shouting. One of them shouted, "Come over and finish it". Our machine gun silenced

them. 7.50am, A German standing on hostile parapet was shot by B Coy sniper.

13.9.1915
9.45am - Our sniper hit a German periscope. 8pm - D Coy on left 1st line trenches opened rapid fire on enemy heard moving in hedge. 9pm - Enemy fired 19 shells behind Reserve Trenches & finally set fire to haystack.
11pm - Having handed over our section of trenches to the South Lancashire Regt., we evacuated & marched to billets at LOCON.

The next few months were spent behind the lines training and preparing for what would be called The Big Push. The commanding officer of the battalion, Lieutenant-Colonel Carton de Wiart, D.S.O, was awarded the Victoria Cross for his action leading the 8th Battalion at La Boiselle, during the Somme offensive. During this battle, Colonel de Wiart, who had lost a hand earlier in the War, was said to have torn out the safety pins of bombs with his teeth, and hurled them at the enemy with his one hand. He had also lost an eye in battle, and wore a black patch. The men called him Nelson.

On the 5th July the battalion withdrew to Albert with 302 casualties. They remained here resting, cleaning equipment and replenishing stores. Oliver had time for a welcome bath. Most soldiers in the frontline had to put up with lice which were itchy and caused sores. A hot bath was a chance to have a good wash and be issued with a fumigated uniform, which kept the lice at bay for a while.

War Diaries 8th Battalion Gloucestershire Regiment

7.7.1916
ALBERT - Under Coy arrangements, baths were arranged for the Bn during the day.

8.7.1916
Bn was inspected by Maj Gen Bridges & complimented on their recent achievements.

Between the 9th July and the 18th July, the battalion spent time on physical drill, Church parades, inspections and route marches at Millencourt. Oliver was back into the old German line near Bazentin-le-Petit on the 20 July 1916 and on the 22 July the battalion attacked the Switch Line which cut through High Wood, but the attack was driven off and the battalion suffered 200 casualties, including Lieut-Colonel de Wiart.

War Diaries 8th Battalion Gloucestershire Regiment

20.7.1916
Moved into the Old German Line close to BAZENTIN-LE-PETIT.

22.7.1916
9.30pm Relieved Worc. R (10th) in front and prepared to attack the German switch line cutting through the north of HIGH WOOD and running S. of MARTINPUICH with 10th R War and 7th S Lanc. 1am Attack failed our casualties being 1 officer killed, 5 wounded, 8 missing including the C.O. Lt Col. de Wiart, gunshot wound in the neck. 186 casualties among other ranks.

The battalion moved to Becourt Wood on 24 July and the next few days were spent refitting and reinforcing the battalion. On the 29 July, the battalion were back in the frontline trenches in front of Bazentin-le-Petit where they relieved 6th Wiltshire Regiment. The 8th Glosters cut the wire in front of their own line preparatory to attacking the enemy. On the 30 July, under a cover of a smoke screen Oliver, along with the Brigade, attacked the Intermediate Line at High Wood. The 8th Glosters and 10th Worcesters went forward but were stopped by heavy machine-gun fire and concealed snipers, and had to withdraw with heavy losses. Total casualties were around 170 men. This was the day that Oliver lost his life.

War Diaries 8th Battalion Gloucestershire Regiment

30.7.1916
6.10pm Attacked the German Intermediate line, A & B Coys in frontline, C & D Coys in second line. Our attack was held up by enfilade Machine Gun

fire and concealed snipers from our right. Our men returned to their original frontline at 9.30pm

Casualties: Officers, 8 killed, 3 wounded, 3 missing, the CO Maj. Thynne was wounded in the body while urging on the second line. Other Ranks 160 killed

The Commonwealth War Graves Commission gives details of the attack as follows.

> 'On 1 July 1916, supported by a French attack to the south, thirteen divisions of Commonwealth forces launched an offensive on a line from north of Gommecourt to Maricourt. Despite a preliminary bombardment lasting seven days, the German defences were barely touched and the attack met unexpectedly fierce resistance. Losses were catastrophic and with only minimal advances on the southern flank, the initial attack was a failure. In the following weeks, huge resources of manpower and equipment were deployed in an attempt to exploit the modest successes of the first day. However, the German Army resisted tenaciously and repeated attacks and counter attacks meant a major battle for every village, copse and farmhouse gained. At the end of September, Thiepval was finally captured. The village had been an original objective of 1 July. Attacks north and east continued'

Oliver's mother received a letter of sympathy from 2/Lt Pope, the officer in charge of Oliver's section, who was to be awarded the Distinguished Service Order in 1917.

> 'Dear Mrs Porter
> It is with very much regret that I write to inform you of the death in action of your son, Private O. J. Porter, No 13647, at Bazentin, on 30th of last month. Your son was a keen, smart, and a good soldier, and very efficient as a machine-gunner, being one of my no. 1's, and was very popular in the section. At the taking of Boiselle, although his gun was blown up and some of his team killed by a shell, and he himself badly bruised

and knocked about, yet he continued for two days to carry out his duties in a most satisfactory manner.

Yours sincerely
Edward B Pope
Second-Lieutenant M.G.O., Gloucester Regiment, 8th Brigade'

A memorial service was also held for Oliver in St John the Baptist's Church, Great Rissington, which was reported in the local paper.

Wiltshire and Gloucestershire Standard 19th August 1916

MEMORIAL SERVICE
A service in memoriam was again held in the church of St John the Baptist on Sunday last after Evensong. A good arrangement as it gave the whole congregation a fitting opportunity of showing their sympathy. The centre of sorrow on this occasion was Mr O. J. Porter of the Gloucester Regiment who has sacrificed his life for his king and country and his friends.

Oliver's body was never found and he is commemorated on the Thiepval Memorial to the missing. His photo also appears on the panel of 600 missing in the visitors centre. The memorial at Thiepval, designed by Sir Edward Lutyens, is built on the highest point on the Somme and can be seen from almost everywhere on the old battlefield. It has the names of over 72,000 missing British and South African men carved into its stone panels who have no known grave.

Oliver's name carved into the memorial

Charles Pratley

20373 Lance Corporal C Pratley
Gloucestershire Regiment

CHARLES WILLIAM PRATLEY was born in 1877 in Leafield, Oxfordshire, the son of Walter and Thirza Pratley. Charles left school aged 13 and started work on a farm in Leafield. In 1900 he married Annie Hopkins, a local girl and moved to Alexandra Street, Birmingham where he worked for Great Western Railways as a Railway Carter. Charles and Annie had five children by 1905, Emily, Henry, Evelyn, Elsie and Alice.

By 1911, the family had moved to Swinford Lodge, Eynsham, Oxfordshire where Charles worked as a Gamekeeper. Just before the war, Charles took another gamekeeping job and the family moved to a cottage in Barrington Bushes, a wood within the parish of Great Rissington. Charles and Annie's daughter, Alice, married Jack Pratley after the war, (no relation). Jack features in another chapter in this book.

When war broke out in 1914, Charles had already been a member of the Territorial Force (TF), known as Saturday Night Soldiers. This was a sort of Home Guard and men were not expected to serve abroad. The men of the TF came from all walks of life and trained a couple of nights a week. They also went on an annual camp, much the same as the T.A. do today. Even so, when war was declared, the majority signed up for overseas duty and units were soon mobilised and in the frontline. Although Charles had been out of the TF for some years he wanted to do his bit and immediately volunteered. He enlisted into the 7th (Service) Battalion Gloucestershire Regiment, on 14 April 1915 at Stow on the Wold at the age of 37. The 7th Gloucester Battalion saw action in Egypt June 1915, Gallipoli July 1915, and Mesopotamia February 1916.

The Gallipoli Campaign was fought between the Turkish and Germans on one side and the British, Australian, New Zealander, Indian and South African allied with the French and Senegal armies on the other. It lasted about nine months and cost the lives of over 500,000 men. Conditions at Gallipoli were horrendous. The land and the close proximity of the fighting made it difficult for proper burials. The heat caused illness, owing to the large number of flies and vermin. 145,000 casualties were caused by illness including, diarrhoea and dysentery.

Charles sailed from England in June 1915, and landed in Gallipoli in July 1915. On 7 August 1915, the battle of Chunuk Bair began. By the following day, there were only 181 men alive or unwounded out of 1000 of those who had advanced. General Sir Ian Hamilton in his famous Dardanelles dispatch wrote:

> *"Chunuk Bair - The 7th Glosters suffered terrible losses here. The fire was so hot that they never got a chance to dig their trenches deeper than some six inches, and where they had to withstand attack after attack. Every single officer, Company Sergeant Major, or Company Quartermaster Sergeant was either killed or wounded. Here is one instance where a Battalion of the New Army fought right on, from mid-day to sunset, without any officers."*

CHARLES PRATLEY

It was here that Charles suffered a wound and ended up back in England to recuperate.

Charles front left in his 'Hospital Blue' uniform

After recovering from his wound, Charles returned home for some leave before returning to Gallipoli sometime in September 1915.

On the 26 November, there was a tremendous rainstorm, which completely flooded the trenches of the allies and enemy alike. This was followed by blizzards, snow and two nights of bitter frost. Many men drowned or were frozen to death by the cold. During the next three days, there were over 5000 cases of frostbite.

War Diaries 7th Battalion Gloucestershire Regiment

SUVLA BAY, GALLIPOLI trenches and corresponding support and reserve trenches.

26.11.1915
At about 1830 a rainstorm coming with great rapidity and violence, burst over our lines. As a result, the ground between our firing line and that of the enemy quickly became the bed of a large lake, The weight and volume of which proved too great for our parapets, and the water pouring in soon rendered our trenches untenable. The troops occupying the trenches at the time dug themselves in behind the parados. Capt A Clark, however, still kept

communication clear with the 7th N Staffs Regt on our right and the Lancs Fus. Regt on our left. Lieut Rathbone, 2/Lt R F Scammell and 2/Lt A Lewis kept communications open between the firing, support and reserve trenches. The flood destroyed much property, equipment etc. and carried away or destroyed most of the Bn and Coy records. (Note no effective strength return since the end of October).

By March 1916, the 7th Glosters had moved to Egypt but the battalion was still not at full fighting strength.

War Diaries 7th Battalion Gloucestershire Regiment 2nd to 31st April

Effective strength: 28 Officers and 731 Other Ranks

8.4.1916
Bn marched to MARGHIL No.3 berth and embarked on a river steamer.

11.4.1916
Reached AMARAH , tied up for the night. One man lost overboard during night.

15.4.1916
Reached OSAH. Bn disembarked and pitched camp 400yds from river bank.

17.4.1916
Received orders to embark at 7.30pm. P.I. Camp was struck and baggage immediately moved to jetty. Owing to lack of orders and slowness, could not sail till 2am

18.4.1916
Reached corps HQ & disembarked about 6am All the heavy kits were unloaded on barge 81. In fact Bn was continually on fatigue until 8.15pm when it marched to DHQ arriving there about 1.30am. Bn was put into very badly constructed reserve trench.

19.4.1916
In spite of the fact the Bn was worn out, having been on continuous fatigue for 36 hours, to get any cover at all, it had to continue digging till daylight.

At 6.45am our artillery started a heavy bombardment to cover attack of our infantry, on the BEIT AIESSA position. Turks replied with shrapnel. Very well aimed and well burst over our reserve trenches and in the first hour Bn suffered 50 casualties. About 9am orders were received for C Coy to reinforce Worcesters and R Warwicks. We were out of touch of C Coy by orderly and wire until 2pm when messages were received via 9th Worcs. During the advance OC C Coy Lt F L C Hodson was wounded and also 2Lt K Ford. C Coy joined the Bn at 11pm.

Cas: killed 12, wounded 71, missing 16, died of wounds 4

20.4.1916
Orders were rec'd from 39th Bde about 7pm to push forward during the night and join N Staffs at A4. A Coy was detailed for this purpose with D Coy to follow as a digging party to make communication trench between PIMPLES and A4 if attack succeeded. B & C Coy's were detailed by 39th to dig another communication trench along stream towards A3. At 11pm A Coy moved out and shortly afterwards came under heavy machine gun fire from Turkish trenches. This Coy contrived its advance over the first line of enemy's trench but again meeting heavy fire and bombs from Turkish communication. Trench A12 were forced to withdraw losing heavily in doing so.. It was here that OC A Coy Capt G B Rathbone was killed and 2Lt W D Bourton who had been attached to A Coy in charge of bombers was also killed. D Coy was pushed up in support losing in doing so Capt Scamell…… In the mean time B & C Coys had been brought up from the right and were sent forward with tools to make an attempt to work on the comm. trench. The result of the nights work was the digging of a communication trench between the point A4 and halfway to the pimples.

Cas: killed O-0, OR-6, wounded O-0, OR-77, missing OR-35, died of wounds OR-1

Charles suffered a further wound to his right arm and was sent to Ingram Road War Hospital, Croydon to recover, but owing to complications and damage to his arm, he was discharged from active service. His Commanding Officer gave the following account about Charles.

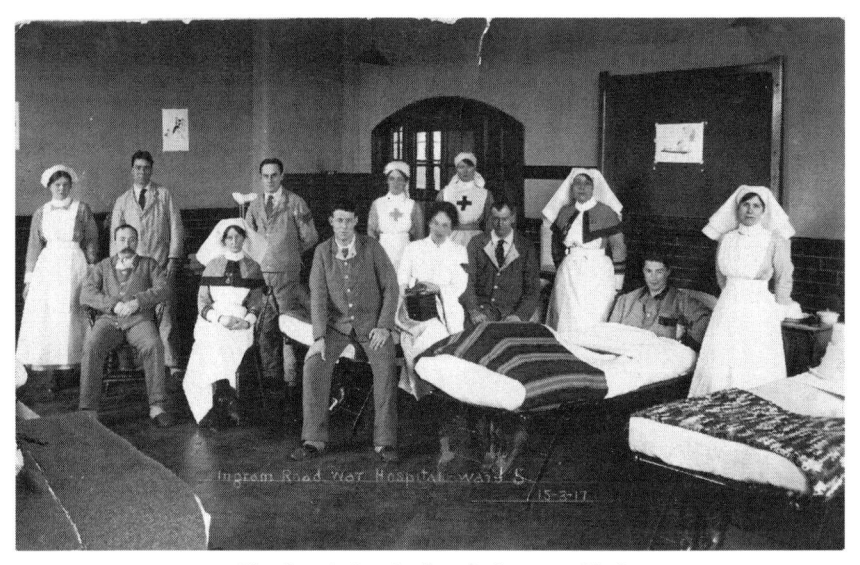

Charles sitting in the chair second left

'Has a very good character. Steady and well conducted'

In 1917, Charles became a member of The Royal Defence Corps (RDC), serving at home. The RDC was formed in August 1917 and made up from soldiers who were over the age for fighting and men who were no longer fit for war duty owing to wounds from active service. The RDC was similar to the Home Guard in the Second World War and guarded railways, ports etc.

On 19 February 1919, Charles was demobilised and went back to Barrington bushes to take up his old job as Gamekeeper. He can be seen on the demob photo, second right in the front row wearing his Royal Defence Corps badge on his lapel. Charles died in 1932 aged 55 and is buried in St John the Baptist's Churchyard Extension, Great Rissington.

The Pratley Boys

JOHN WILLIAM AND Robert Pratley lived in Great Rissington, with their Parents Fred and Emma (nee Ruck). There were ten children in the family with Jack born in 1897 and Bob in 1899. An older brother, Albert, had died in 1891 and their parents had named another son in his memory in 1907.

Jack left school at 13 and started working as a ploughboy on one of the farms. Both boys served with the Worcestershire Regiment during the war. Jack joined up in 1915 under the Derby Scheme and Bob was to follow his brother in 1917 when he was still underage.

Jack Pratley

187301 Pte J W Pratley Worcestershire Regiment

JACK ENLISTED ON 30 Aug 1915 and joined the 3rd battalion Worcestershire Regiment. He was 19 years old. He probably went to France sometime in October, joining the battalion towards the end of the Somme offensive. The battalion were in front line trenches near La Boiselle, Ovillers area.

Towards the end of the month Jack moved to Doullens and entrained for Belgium moving into the Ploegsteert sector, known as Plug Street to the Tommies. The rest area was known as the Piggeries. This was just behind Ploegsteert Wood, where there were several farms, which the troops used as billets. The Piggeries was a building in which it was said the King of Belgium had kept pigs. It had two rows of sties built from concrete in which the men slept on straw. Quite a cushy billet during the war!

Jack had a relatively quiet few months alternating between reserve, support and frontline duty. He frequently took park in raids at night on the enemy's trenches in order to take prisoners and find out about the German positions.

War Diaries 3rd Battalion Worcestershire Regiment

2.6.1917

10.45pm. The attacking troops formed up in their lines in front of our parapet and awaited the firing of our barrage.

10.50pm. ZERO. An intense barrage was opened on the enemy's frontlines and strong points in rear which lifted at zero+2. The enemy's frontline was immediately entered. Some resistance was offered which was speedily overcome by the resolution of our troops and the entire enemy encountered were either killed or taken prisoner. The advance was then continued in accordance with plan and at zero+7 NUTMEG SUPPORT was raided. At the junction of NUTMEG AVE and NUTMEG SUPPORT and enemy machine gun opened fire. This was immediately attacked with bombs and the team fled. No prisoners were taken in this line. Some Germans were seen running away as our men entered. At zero+19 our troops withdrew from German trenches and under cover of our artillery barrage returned to our own lines. Twelve prisoners were brought back to our trenches, three others being killed crossing 'no man's land'. To the most part the enemy showed little inclination to fight and appeared glad to be taken. Casualties were 3 OR killed and 10 wounded. Most of which were slight. The raid was entirely successful. Congratulatory messages were received from the Corps and Divisional Commanders

Raids of this kind took place in a prelude to the Battle of Messines. The main attack took place on 7 June 1917 when 19 mines were detonated along a nine-mile front causing the largest explosion in history. On 6 June under the cover of darkness, Jack and his battalion moved into the assembly trenches ready to go over the top. At 3.10am the mines were detonated and shook the ground as the whistles blew.

War Diaries 3rd Battalion Worcestershire Regiment

7.6.1917

3.30am. Zero hour. Under cover of the greatest weight of activity ever employed in battle, the Bn. left its positions of assembly and moved forward to the assault. At the same moment many mines were sprung under the enemy frontline. The magnitude of the mining operations were not made known to *our own troops prior to zero hour and consequently the sudden firing of so many large mines had momentarily a bad effect on them. During the initial attack the Bn. had on its right flank the 13th Cheshire Regt, 74th Inf. Bde. and on the left the 8th Royal North Lancashire Regt. C Coy on the right and B Coy on the left entered NUTMEG TRENCH at zero+3½ minutes. No serious opposition encountered. At zero +7 min NUTMEG RESERVE was captured. D Coy and A Coy moved forward in succession immediately behind C & B Coy. Battalion H Q were in rear of A Coy. D Coy then went forward and captured the line BELL FARM which objective was taken at zero+20.*

3.30 am Strong concrete dugouts which had withstood the bombardment was found on this line. They contained about sixty Germans who would not come out until bombs had been hurled inside. Some enemy were killed in this fighting. The remainder were made prisoners. From the beginning of the assault owing to the darkness at the time of launching the attack and almost unrecognisable state of the ground, direction was lost by most units in the proximity early in the advance and regiments became very mixed. Throughout the whole of the attack the men had shown the greatest eagerness to press forward and there is little doubt that some of them of them ran into our barrage.

Jack and his battalion had to endure some close hand to hand fighting but took 40 prisoners and a further 60 from the captured dugouts. Even though the attack was a complete success, 10 officers and 230 men had been killed or were wounded or missing. On 11 June the battalion was relieved and went into reserve trenches. At the end of June Jack was back in billets for a period of training and rest.

The third battle of Ypres, also known as Passchendaele began in July 1917. Jack moved to Poperinge by motorbus on the 6 July 1917 and then marched to Ypres into billets at the Lille Gate. Over 900 buses were used to move troops during the First World War. They were painted khaki and their windows were boarded with planks for protection.

Jack had a few days rest in Ypres and returned to the trenches at Hooge on the 21 July. Over the next four days, the battalion sent out patrols into the enemy trenches to try to capture prisoners who could give information on enemy activity. All men had to take turns doing this very dangerous work and no doubt Jack would have taken part in such an activity. Patrols went out at night when it was dark and quiet and would inch forward across no man's land on their stomachs. Raiding parties were also undertaken, with men carrying homemade coshes and grenades. The most dangerous part of a trench raid or patrol was returning to your own lines when you could be fired on by your own men.

War Diaries 3rd Battalion Worcestershire Regiment

21.7.1917
2nd Lt A R Ping and 12 OR's who formed part of a patrol which entered the enemy trenches near the HOOGE CRATER, with the intention of remaining all night, failed to return, having apparently lost their way and fallen into enemy hands.

22.7.1917
Patrols were sent out each night, which entered the enemy frontline trenches without encountering any Germans.

On the 31 July, Jack with the 3rd Worcesters was in forward dugouts at a position called Halfway House. The battle of Passchendaele was about to begin. The battalion spent five days in heavy rain and continuous shellfire with ground turning to mud, which was knee deep. The Germans fired gas shells and the battalion lost almost a quarter of its strength.

After a brief rest period behind the lines, Jack returned to frontline duties on the 9 August. The battle was still underway and Jack's battalion would be attacking the enemy the following day. After dark, the men moved into the support trenches they had held the week before. On the 10 August, the British artillery opened fire and Jack charged forward in the sticky mud.

War Diaries 3rd Battalion Worcestershire Regiment

10.8.1917
3am – Bn on BELLEWARDE RIDGE moved up to WESTHOEK RIDGE to

support 13th Cheshire Regt who were taking part in an attack on the BLACK LINE.

4am – *Attack launched provoking enemy artillery on WESTHOEK and BELLEWARDE RIDGE and intervening ground.*

7am – *74 Inf Bde gained all their objectives. Bn HQ and remaining two Coys moved to the right end of WESTHOEK RIDGE, which was being very heavily shelled. The battalion suffered considerable losses during the morning. Total casualties during the day. Officers, one killed, two wounded. Ordinary Ranks, 10 killed, 41 wounded.*

All German counter-attacks were fended off and as darkness fell the men held on to the ridge. The next day, the defence of the ridge carried on. The battalion Chaplain was killed and the Medical Officer was wounded and later died.

11.8.1917
Bn remained on WESTHOEK RIDGE supporting the 13th Cheshires who had lost very heavily and assisting them in holding the new line gained. During the morning the Rev G M Evans who had been attached to the Bn for 2½ years as Chaplain and who was immensely beloved by all ranks, was killed.

Jack's battalion was relieved the following night and they withdraw having lost a third of their men. It had been a successful operation despite the severe cost of lives. The men moved into rest areas and spent the remainder of 1917 in a relatively quiet sector.

In July 1918, A signal was received by Jack's Division and read out to the troops.

> *"Reserve Army Special Order*   G.A. 31/4/1
> *25th Division G 22/88*
>
> *The Commander of the reserve army wishes to express his high appreciation of the excellent work which they have done while under his command. They have been engaged day and night against a brave and determined enemy, who has had every advantage of ground, and by their perseverance*

and endurance they have done much to facilitate the task of the troops on their right. Progress has been steady, and the results achieved have been of great value to our cause at these Divisions"

By September 1918, Jack was holding the line with his battalion and about to take part in the capture of a heavily fortified enemy redoubt.

War Diaries 3rd Battalion Worcestershire Regiment

25.9.1918
3am Bttn. relieved the 8th Gloucester's in right sub-sector prior to attacking SHEPHERD REDOUBT and the DISTILLERY. All objectives captured, about 80 prisoners and 10 machine guns captured. Our casualties slight. Final lines ran about 50yds east of the LA BASSEE ROAD.
6pm Very heavy barrage put down just behind our frontline. Enemy immediately attempted to counter-attack, but was scattered by our rifle and Lewis guns. Our men advanced from their trenches to meet the enemy and to escape the barrage. Our line absolutely intact. Quiet night ensued.

26.9.1918
3.30am Enemy again attempted to counter-attack and was again repulsed by the rifle and Lewis gun-fire. For the remainder of the day no infantry actions developed but artillery was active on both sides. 1st/Lt. G. T. Brush MC and 2nd/ Lt. B. Newcastle were wounded during the day. Bttn. was relieved and handed over the line intact to 8th Gloucs during night.

After the capture of Shepherd's redoubt a message was sent to be read out to the troops;

'September 28th 1918
Messages published for information and communication to all ranks

"Please convey my hearty congratulations to Lt. Col. WHALLEY and all ranks of the Worcestershire Regiment on *their fine performance in capturing Shepherds Redoubt and the Distillery and holding them against all counter attacks."*

*Signed G. D. Jeffreys Major General
Commanding Division'*

After the signing of the Armistice on 11 November 1918, Jack moved to billets at Le Cateau and began salvage work. By 1 of March, all men who had enlisted before January 1916 were sent home to be demobilised.

Jack had been in some heavy action and some major battles but he was fortunate and survived the war. He came back home to Great Rissington and married Alice Pratley (Charles Pratley's daughter) in 1927 and they lived at The Bank. They had two children, Philip and Sheila who still live locally today. Jack worked as a security man at Little Rissington Aerodrome for many years until he retired. He died in Burford Hospital in 1967 aged 70 and is buried in St John the Baptist's Churchyard Extension, Great Rissington.

Jack and Alice on their wedding day. Charles Pratley is standing to the right of the bride.

Bob Pratley

43321 Private R Pratley Worcestershire Regiment

BOB PRATLEY ATTESTED at Stow on the Wold in February 1917 joining the 1st battalion Gloucestershire Regiment. Bob probably lied about his age to get in because he was still only 17 years old. Bob did his basic training and had the photo below taken to send home to his mother.

Bob (centre) and some pals at training camp

Bob was transferred to the Worcestershire Regiment on his arrival at Etaples, France. The Worcesters probably needed new drafts to cover their losses, and Bob joined the 1st battalion at Amiens. Bob would soon be in the trenches but the beginning of

April saw him training in the reserve lines and taking part in sports programmes.

War Diaries 1st Battalion Worcestershire Regiment

Amiens
1-4.3.1918
Bn billeted in JUNCTION CAMP. Working parties found daily for RUPPRECHT KEEP and GREY RUIN.

5-12.3.1918
Bn entrained at WIELTIE, detrained ABEELE and marched to WATOU where a programme of training was carried out as laid down until 12th incl. Boxing contest was held during the period.

13.3.1918
Bn marched to ABEELE and entrained there for LUMBRES – after detraining, the Bn marched to MORINGHEM where it was in GHQ reserve.

21.3.1918
Training was carried out as laid down in programme, boxing contests were held and cross country runs were organised during the period.

22.3.1918
Bn proceeded by route march from MORINGHEM to St OMER where it entrained for NESTLE.

23.3.1918
Bn detrained at NESTLE at 2.30am marched to EPEMANCOURT. Position was taken up by Bn along the W Bank of canal, the right of Bn resting on PARGNY. In the afternoon A & B Coys took up position E of FALVY and fought rearguard action to extricate another division. FALVY was then evacuated and former positions on canal reoccupied. The enemy at about 9.40pm entered EPEMANCOURT but was ejected by a swift counter attack lead by the Lt Col Roberts.

24.3.1918
The right flank of the Bde on right was forced back and in time the Bn was forced back to LICOURT where a position was held E of that village.

25.3.1918
After very severe fighting the Bn was forced to retire and took up position on the Rly line S of MARCHELPOT, which was held. Before midnight the Bn was ordered to retire on to works E of ABLAINCOURT.

26.3.1918
The enemy came on again soon after daylight and invested the works at ABLAINCOURT, the right flank having given the Bde retired via LIHONS (the enemy was then in possession of CHAULINES to RISIERES where a position was taken up SE of that village between RELY and the road junction S E of POSIERES. The enemy invested this position in the afternoon.

27.3.1918
The enemy attacked at 6.30am and the line was very hard pressed, but a counter attack from the right enabled us to retake a few posts occupied by the enemy. This line was held throughout the day after very severe fighting.

28.3.1918
After severe fighting the Bn retired and took up a position on the high ground N W of VRELY. The enemy having entered VRELY, the Bn subsequently retired on to a position on the high ground S E of CAIX. The Bn was then ordered to evacuate this line and proceeded to MUREUIL then to ROUVREL where it was billeted for the night. Total Cas: Officers killed 2, wounded 18. Other Ranks killed 24, wounded 174, missing 200

From 18 March to 22 March, Bob was behind the lines and took part in a training programme with his battalion, to prepare for further frontline duties.

'TIL THE BOYS COME HOME

War Diaries 1st Battalion Worcestershire Regiment

Training programme for the period Monday 18th to Saturday 22nd March.

18th   Whole day on range
19th   Drill order parades with steady drill
20th   Route march
21st   Musketry, bombing, muscle exercises, lecture on night operations
22nd   Lewis gun and rifle training
Daily orders
Reveille 6.45am, Breakfast 7.45am, Dinners 1pm, Lights out at 9.10pm, Sundays will be a day of rest.

By August, Bob and his battalion had moved forward again into the frontline trenches

War Diaries 1st Battalion Worcestershire Regiment

1.8.1918
Bn. in TRENCHES MERICOURT sector Attitude of enemy very quiet. Enemy carried out shelling attack. Casualties 7 Off 31 OR

2.8.1918
As above. Enemy aeroplane brought down by L G fire. 6 OR's gassed

8.8.1918
In camp day devoted to general cleaning up. His Majesty the King passed through MONT ST ETOY in the afternoon. Bn joined the route.

16.8.1918
Bn embarked at 4pm and relieved the 6th Highland Light Inf in the OPPY sector. Relief completed by 9.30pm Sector very quiet

26.8.1918
From dusk Two Coys were working on a scheme of outposts when orders were received to send out patrols and find out where the enemy was. After this patrol had gone, orders received to establish ourselves in enemy's system.

A Coy did the patrol and established themselves in AREUX LOOP south. D Coy then followed and bombed to the south. Very serious opposition was met in SEVERN ALLEY when a block was made and this position was held. B Coy then went in further south. Via MACHINE GUN Trench and TOMMY ALLEY and established themselves in TOMMY ALLEY. Bombed up Z Trench and TOMMY Trench but could only get about half way up the trenches where blocks were formed and positions held on to. A Coy Patrol with-drawn. A & C Coys ordered to occupy BOW Trench and support respectively. Casualties 10 Off and 6 OR wounded, 10 OR Killed, 2OR gassed. During the morning the whole of ARLEUX LOOP South and 2 trench made good and orders received to push on further at the same time side slipping to the south. D Coy relieved and ordered back to Bow support, C Coy ordered forward to Bow Trench and ordered to carry out bombing attacks, objectives whole system on Bn Front. This was carried out and final objectives gained without serious opposition. The enemy then tried four times to bomb us out coming from Albert but our positions were held.
 Casualties OR- killed 1, wounded 11, gassed 1.

Bob served with the 1st battalion Worcesters until the end of the war, and came through unscathed. He was demobilised early in 1919. In 1922 he married Annie Kight and they had eight children, living in Sherborne Lane.

Bob helped build the Model Village in Bourton on the Water and then later worked at Little Rissington Aerodrome as a Security Man with his brother Jack. Bob can be seen in the demob photo standing 2nd left and also in the parade photo last man at the back with the flat cap. He died in 1959 and is buried in Great Rissington churchyard, where his headstone simply says *'Our Dad'*.

Joyce Coles with her dad Bob

George Rachael

20023 Pte G H Rachael MM Gloucestershire Regt

GEORGE HERBERT RACHAEL was the fourth son of Philip and Georgina Rachael, born in Oddington in 1894. He was one of 14 children, and in 1901 the family lived in Eyford, Nr Lower Slaughter, where his father was a cowman on a farm. He had three other brothers, Joseph, John and Ernest, who also fought in the war, one of whom was killed on the Somme, in 1916.

George was working as a Carter when he attested to the Gloucestershire Regiment on 7 April 1915 joining at Bristol. He was subsequently posted to the 3rd Battalion on 12 April 1915. The 3rd Glosters remained in Britain throughout the war, providing drafts to other Battalions. On 15 May, George transferred to the 1st (Home Service) Garrison Battalion Middlesex Regiment. He was appointed unpaid Lance Corporal and was based at Chatham Docks to guard the Thames Estuary and the dockyard defences. On the 15 August 1917 George was transferred back to the 3rd Glosters and left for France arriving at No 55 *Infantry Base Depot* in Etaples. This was a holding camp where men continued training in trench warfare until they were posted to the front. After a period of training George was drafted into the 12th Glosters, also known as Bristol's Own, and left Rouen for frontline duty.

*A Gloucestershire Regiment battalion marching through a French town
Courtesy of The Soldiers of Gloucestershire Museum*

In mid September George continued his training with the 12th Glosters at Maizieres where he did physical drill and musketry. The battalion also took part in a practice attack with battalions from other regiments acting as the enemy.

War Diaries 12th Battalion Gloucestershire Regiment

*21.9.1917
Lecture by Captain W.G. Chapman M.C. at 9.30am. A performance was given by the WHIZZ BANGS (Divisional Concert Party) in MAIZIERES at 10.30am. Battalion paraded at 3.20pm for night operations and marched to GRAND RULLECOURT. Bn. in support for an attack on German trenches.*

*"The Whizz-Bangs". 12th Battalion, The Gloucestershire Regiment. c.1916
Courtesy of Soldiers of Gloucestershire Museum*

On the 1 October 1917, George and the 12th Glosters moved to Meteren, Flanders. The Third Battle of Ypres was launched on 31 July, also known as Passchendaele. This was to be one of the most appalling battles of World War One. The summer of 1917 was unusually cold and wet, and the ground turned into a quagmire. Many soldiers simply disappeared in liquid mud filled craters. About 300,000 allied soldiers became casualties at Passchendaele, with many having no known grave. The ground to be covered was only 8000 yards with the battle resulting in 37 men lost for every yard gained.

War Diaries 12th Battalion Gloucestershire Regiment

1.10.1917
METEREN
The battalion paraded at 6.30am and proceeded to frontline to relieve 11th Bn. W.Yorks Regt. (68th Infy. Bde.) who were in reserve. Relief completed by 9am. Position of Companies was as follows :-
"B" Company on left. FITZCLARENCE FARM
"C" Company on right. ROUND CHATEAU
"A" Company in left support. WEST INVERNESS COPSE (sic)

"D" Company in right support WEST INVERNESS COPSE
Bn. H.Q. CLAPHAM JUNCTION
Bn. was in support to 7 E. Surrey Regt.
There was heavy shelling by the enemy during the night and S.O.S. rockets were sent up on several occasions during the night.
4 O.R. Casualties.

2.10.1917
In Reserve
Battalion in Reserve. Companies were consolidating and improving the trench as far as possible during the day. The Companies in right support positions very badly drawn the enemy's Gas Shells. 2/Lt J. A. Baerdrick, 2/Lt H. Wood and 2/Lt L. C. May were gassed and the battalion lost about 100 O.R., the majority of which were Gassed.

3.10.1917
Battalion in Reserve. Improvement of positions continue. Enemy's artillery was still very active. Preparations for advance were being carried out. Nothing of importance for report.
Casualties were 2/Lt N. C. B. Bloodworth Gassed and 30 O.R.

4.10.1917
Battalion was in reserve to 1/E Surrey Regt during an attack on the enemy line by the Second Army. 95th Infy. Bde. was on the left of the Divisional front with 1/Devons on the right and 1/D.O.L.I. on the left with the 1/E. Surreys in close support and 12th Bn. Gloucestershire Regt in support to 1/E. Surreys. The 2/KOSB's attacked on the right of 1/Devons, with 64th Infy. Brigade on the left.
The attack commenced at 6am and at 6.40am the battalion less "A" Company (which had been detailed for carrying) moved forward to secure the line held by 7/E Surrey Regt through JUT FARM as follows.

"B" & "D" Companies both N. of REUTAL BEEK ("B" on the left). Companies had very heavy casualities in moving into new positions and intense artillery was very active during these operations. At 10.10 am orders were received to send "C" Coy (which was on the right) forward to reinforce 1/Devon Regt.

GEORGE RACHAEL

The casualties were very heavy during these operations. 2/Lt J. F. Hanstone and 2/Lt D. W. Bailey were killed. Captain C. S. Pretheran, 2/Lt H. B. McShane and 2/Lt F. H. Andrews - wounded. Total casualties O.R. 150

It was reported in the local paper that George was wounded in action on 3 October 1917 but it's likely it was during the action in the early hours of the 4 October. George had suffered a gunshot wound to his right thigh. He was sent back to Blighty to recover and returned to the front on 12 January 1918.

In early August 1918, George was awarded a Military Medal during an act of gallantry where he saved a wounded man. According to family members, George carried the wounded man out of the battlefield and then for a further three miles even though he had been shot himself with the bullet passing through his mouth and out through the side of his face. He was to carry the scar for the rest of his life. He was gazetted on 7 October 1918, about the same time as the 12th Battalion were disbanded.

George was sent home to England to recuperate and during this leave he married Florence James in St John the Baptist's Church, Great Rissington. He returned to the front on 2 November 1918 where he was posted to the 1st battalion Glosters and remained with this battalion until he was demobbed.

George and Florence went on to have 15 children, two of whom died in infancy. George can be seen in the 1937 Coronation Parade photo 3rd from the back wearing his military medal. He died in 1961 and is buried in the village churchyard alongside Florence.

Percy Smith

23783 Pte P J Smith Gloucestershire Regiment

PERCY SMITH WAS born in Turkdean in 1880, the son of Lawrence and Sophia Smith who managed Church Farm. In 1905, Percy married Florence Clifford from Idbury and they moved to Witts Farm in Over Norton where their four sons were born; Percy, John, Lawrence and Maurice. By 1915, Percy, Florence and the boys had moved to The Haven, Great Rissington where Percy rented some land to farm.

On 25 July 1915, Percy volunteered for War Service and attested at Stow on the Wold where he joined the 10th (Service) Battalion Gloucestershire Regiment. He left Great Rissington on 2 August 1915 and joined his battalion in Cheltenham, training on nearby Cleeve Hill. On 8 August Percy embarked on a ship at Southampton for Le Havre, France.

Percy took part in the Battle of Loos, which began on 25 September 1915 and was one of the first major battles on the Western Front. It was also the first time gas was used by the Allies.

'TIL THE BOYS COME HOME

War Diaries 10th (Service) Battalion Gloucestershire Regiment

24.9.1915
Moved up into battle position at 7.30pm. Black Watch coming in as supporting battalion.

25.9.1915
5.30am. The battalion was ordered to deliver an assault on the first line system of the German defences, which included three lines of entrenchments with the primary objective HULLUCH and PUITS. The assault was carried out in 3 lines, frontage being BOIS CARREE. The attack was delivered at 6.30am on 25/9/15 with accompaniment of gas and smoke. The wind was not quite favourable with the result that from the start several men were affected. Notwithstanding this drawback the three lines moved forward punctually to the moment, machine guns accompanying. The Germans wire entanglement, which had been torn into gaps by bombardment proved a considerable obstacle. The wind proving more favourable to the enemy than ourselves in the smoke, direction was not properly maintained, but deflected to the right. <u>Heavy resistance</u> was encountered at the support and reserve German works at the first, the enemy eventually evacuating these positions and retreating towards HULLOCH. Our bombers suffered severely, their bombs in the main refusing to explode, the BROCK lighter having got wet with the rain, which fell in the early morning. Nevertheless, the assault was pushed home with the utmost resolution over the 2nd German line into the third and up the flanking communication trenches eastwards. In this place the Camerons and Black Watch co-operated. The officers fell as the position of their bodies showed, leading their men and 16 out of 21 officers were lost. The bodies of our dead indicated how they died with faces to the enemy. One of our m/c guns was put out of action on coming over the parapet, but 2 other guns reached a point in advance of Point 89, constructed later. The action resulted in many German surrenders and their flight from the position they were forced to evacuate by the rapid and continuous push of the assault. During the night, under heavy rain, unit was reformed, some 60 survivors assembling increasing by 3rd day to 130.

900 men had gone over the top leaving over 500 men dead or wounded. One survivor recalled:

> *"What a sight. Men riddled on the barbed wire....lying about, discoloured through gas, and others gasping for breath.... How many of our lads at Loos had a last fond look at photos of loved ones, and died with them tightly held in their hands?"*

Percy was admitted to a Field Hospital suffering from the effects of gas inhalation. He was later shipped home to England to recover. Florence visited Percy in hospital and later he had a spell of leave with her and the boys before returning to the front.

Florence took up the post of Infants Supplementary Teacher at Great Rissington Board School on 14 February 1916. With the Pupil Teacher, Tom Hyatt having joined up along with other young men, there was a shortage of teachers in the district.

By the summer of 1916, the 10th Glosters were in the Somme sector of the Western Front. Percy was suffering from an abscess on his neck and was again admitted to a Field Hospital on 2 July 1916. He was later transferred to a General Hospital in Boulogne for further treatment and then on to England. Percy was to suffer further ill health with pleurisy possibly brought on by his encounter with gas earlier on. He spent almost a year in and out of hospital but in late May 1917 was fit enough for further active service.

Percy was transferred to the Rifle Brigade and joined No. 3 Company, 7th battalion in France on 17 June 1917. He spent most of July near Auchonvillers doing physical training, bayonet fighting, rifle drill and firing Lewis guns on the range. The battalion took part in the Brigade Sports on 3 July 1917 winning the Brigadiers Prize coming first in rifle grenade throwing, Lewis gun competition, bugle race, physical training, harnessing up limbers, cooking competition, mule race, tilting the bucket and a boat race.

By August, Percy was once again suffering with his health. He was diagnosed with pyrexia otherwise known as Trench Fever, a broad term for casualties with sickness, high temperature, and respiratory symptoms. He was admitted to hospital on 14 September 1917 and shipped home to England on 8 November.

When Percy recovered he was transferred to the Agricultural Labour Corps and remained in England until the end of the war working on the land. On 28 October 1918 Percy reported sick complaining of cold and cramps. He had contracted influenza and was admitted to a hospital in Bath. Spanish Flu killed over 50 million people worldwide between 1918 and 1920. Percy was seriously ill for several weeks and was eventually discharged on 27 January 1919.

The war was over for Percy and he returned home to Great Rissington and his family. Florence continued with her teaching at the school until 31 March 1919. On 4 April 1919, Percy, Florence and the boys left the village moving to Pegglesworth near Andoversford.

The Souls Boys

A Cotswold Family of Heroes.

Few parents in England could have had a more grevious blow than Mr. and Mrs. Souls, of Great Rissington, Bourton-on-the-Water. Four years ago they rejoiced in the possession of five sons, upon whom they could look with pride, and as a sustenance in their old age. All five went to fight their country's battles—three have been killed in action, and the other two have been missing too long, we fear, to hope for their return. 1.—Pte. W. D. Souls, Worcesters. 2.—Pte. Albert Souls, Worcesters. 3.—Pte. Alfred Souls, Cheshires. 4.—Pte. Arthur Souls, Cheshires. 5.—Pte. F. G. Souls, Cheshires.

Cheltenham Chronicle and Gloucestershire Graphic, 8th June 1918

THE SOULS BROTHERS lived in Great Rissington with their parents, William and (Julia) Annie. There were nine children in the family, Frederick 1886 born in Sherborne, Alfred and Arthur 1887 born in Farmington, Kate 1890, Walter 1892, Albert 1895, Hilda 1898, Percy 1901 and Iris 1903 all born in Great Rissington. Fred was *'boots'* at the Rectory when he was 14, and Alfred and Arthur were both working with horses on Manor Farm aged 13. When war came they were all working on the land.

Albert, (known as Bertie or Bert, by his family), and Walter enlisted at Bourton on the Water joining the 2nd Worcestershire Regiment and after the Battle of Loos, both transferred to the Machine Gun Corps and did their training around Bethune, a mining area in Northern France. Bert, the youngest, was the first to enlist and was also the first to be killed.

Fred, Alf and Arthur, enlisted in to the 16th Cheshires, which was a Bantam Battalion for men under 5' 3" Alf and Arthur were identical twins. Born an hour apart, they died five days apart. Fred would be one of the missing who never returned home.

Bert Souls

17208 Private A Souls Machine Gun Corps

BERT, TOGETHER WITH his brother Walter, joined the 2nd Battalion Worcestershire Regiment in 1915. Enlisting at Bourton on the Water, he left for France on 2 June 1915.

The two boys fought in the battle of Loos (25 September to 28 September 1915) where the British suffered over 61,000 casualties. The battle was a complete disaster. Gas was used for the initial assault but the wind blew it back on the British infantry. The artillery had little effect, and many men were mown down by German machine gun fire. The 2nd Worcesters suffered very heavy casualties along the banks of La Bassee Canal. As the men advanced they were forced together trying to avoid craters and the enemy machine guns had an easy target.

Bert and Walter were both members of the 2nd Worcesters machine gun section. Infantry battalions were equipped with four Maxim machine guns. In September 1915, the War Office proposed a formation of a single machine gun company per each Brigade. The two brothers stayed together, both transferring to the Machine Gun Corps in January 1916.

Bert and Walter moved to Bethune, a mining area in Northern France, to carry out training and further instruction on the Vickers machine gun.

War Diaries 5th Brigade Machine Gun Company

1.1.1916 MALANOY FARM

1.1.1916 to 11.1.1916
This period was devoted to organising the Company and carrying out elementary instruction (mechanism etc)

19.1.1916
Training in mechanism, stoppages & smoke helmet drill.

20.1.1916
A class was started consisting of 20 Officers NCOs & men drawn from each of 4 battalions in the Bde. They were instructed in how to load and fire a machine gun. The programme was as follows:

>*9- 9.45 a.m.*
>*Loading and unloading each man to be taught separately using live rounds*

>*10-10.30a.m.*
>*Firing bursts of six rounds. The belt will be marked off in groups of six. The man will require to unload and reload between each burst. 4 bursts per man.*

>*11.15-11.45a.m.*
>*Same as from 10-10.30 six bursts instead of four.*

21.1.1916 to 24.1.1916 Class for Officers NCOs & men of battalions was carried out. Instruction in mechanism, stoppages, semaphore was carried out by the Coy.

By March 1916, Bert and Walter were in the frontline with their machine gun sections, after only two months training, serving alongside their old pals in the 2nd Worcesters.

War Diaries 2nd Battalion Worcestershire Regiment

4.3.1916
Snow all morning, thawed in afternoon

9.3.1916
The Bn relieved The 4th Kings Liverpools, Auchy. Relief completed by 9.30pm.

10.3.1916
The frontline was in very good condition, but the second line was muddy, also parts of the communication trenches. A very quiet day. During the night Machine guns played along the parapet opposite B and C Coys and prevented them wiring. A Coy put out some wire

11.3.1916
Everything was quiet on our Front, but there was a good deal of shelling on our Right near. HOHENZOLLERN REDOUBT. D Coy sent up a platoon to reinforce C Coy, as their line was only weakly held. The bombers were sent to A Coy as a considerable amount of bombing went on our right. A Coy sent out patrols and put out wire.

12.3.1916
Comm. Officers conference was held at Bde HQ at 10.0a.m. The Officers of the 1/6th Scottish Rifles reconnoitred the line during the morning. A Machine Gun loophole was shelled satisfactorily by our Howitzers and the 18 pounders did some wire cutting. About 5p.m. a considerable amount of shelling and bombing started on our right but was apparently only a false alarm. Relief was completed by 9.00a.m. and the Bn. moved into billets in ANNEQUIN S..

14.3.1916
Very heavy fatigues were furnished by the Bn. The men not on fatigue spent the day cleaning

War Diaries 5th Brigade Machine Gun Company

3.3.1916
5th. Bde section of line is known as the ANGRES section.

4.3.1916 to 13.3.1916
Coy in trenches. Nothing unusual occurred during this period. Ordinary 4 day reliefs were carried out under section arrangements. Casualties nil.

14.3.1916
1 other rank killed. Indirect M.G. fire was carried out by 2 guns of H.L.I. on main crossroads in Angres.

That day there was only one casualty. This must have been Bert, who was killed in action, on 14 March 1916. He was only 20 years old and is buried in Bully-Grenay Communal Cemetery, France.

Annie Souls received a letter from the officer in charge of Bert's gun section;

> 'Private Albert Souls was killed on duty with his gun team yesterday morning. He was always a good soldier, and did his duty in an exemplary manner. His loss is greatly felt both by officers and men, amongst whom he was very popular. Please accept the sympathies of all in your bereavement.'

Bert's grave at Bully-Grenay cemetery

Fred Souls

21686 Private F G Souls Cheshire Regiment

FRED ENLISTED AT Stow on the Wold together with his brothers Arthur and Alf, into the 16th Battalion Cheshire Regiment. The battalion was raised in Birkenhead and was a Bantam battalion for men who were under regulation height but otherwise fit for active service.

As the war progressed, it was realised that normal Army regulations over height needed to be adjusted. 3000 men volunteered and were formed into the 1st and 2nd Birkenhead Battalions, later known as the 15th and 16th Cheshire Battalions. Other regiments also recruited Bantam battalions and they were formed into the 35th Division. The Division moved to France early in 1916 and remained on the Western Front for the rest of the war.

Fred's battalion took part in the German retreat to the Hindenberg Line, from 14 March to 5 April 1916 and the 16th Cheshires also fought in the first battle of the Somme, with devastating losses. On 16 July 1916, the 16th Cheshires went into the frontline between Guillemont and Delville Wood, in the south of the Somme battlefield, at a position known as Waterlot Farm. There was fierce fighting around Waterlot Farm, which was a sugar refinery near Trones Wood.

War Diaries 16th Battalion Cheshire Regiment

16.7.1916
Attached to 54th Bde. Marched at 8.40p.m. to take up line at TRONES WOOD. Took over line at 5.20a.m. A very trying march in heavy rain, through very wet communication trench carrying heavy loads.

A German counter-attack was launched on 18 July and was forced back but with heavy casualties. The next day, there was systematic German shelling which caused many casualties. Between 18 and 20 July, the 16th Cheshires repelled three counter attacks by the enemy and two attempts to capture their trench.

War Diaries 16th Battalion Cheshire Regiment

16th to 19th
Operations in connection with holding line at Trones Wood, Waterlot Farm – Disposition
  Right Coy's Z and Right centre Y digging themselves into shell holes in front of Trones Wood and connecting these up – Supports in deep German dugouts in the wood. – Left centre Coy (X) had two platoons in communication trenches north point of Trones Wood, with two platoons in support behind NW corner of Trones Wood. Left Coy (W) from here to junction of comm. trenches, with one platoon on strong point. Each Coy had its two Lewis guns and four Vickers guns were disposed along the front. On the morning of the 17th July, orders were received from the 54th Bde to take over Waterlot Farm. This could not be done until 12.30 a.m.
  On the 18th owing to a heavy bombardment by enemy artillery all along the line – Waterlot Farm was eventually taken over and garrisoned by W Coy under Lt Ryalls – Every effort was made to improve and wire the whole line but the only opportunity for wiring was between 5.20am on the 17th and midday the same day. At all other times the whole line was bombarded, the bombardment at times being intense and only short spells of work in the open

could be managed. On the morning of the 18th, the garrison of Waterlot Farm did excellent work in strengthening their position. At 2pm the bombardment increased in intensity – at 3pm Lt Ryalls reported the enemy preparing to attack Waterlot Farm. He reported enemy creeping up the railway embankment from the direction of Guillemont.

He sent forward a party with bombs and a Lewis gun to a brick wall which ran parallel to the line of the enemies advance. Enemy got close under the wall but he bombed them out and turned his Lewis gun on the enemy as they returned down the railway embankment. This was the advance guard to a party of 300 of the enemy with two machine guns which advanced along the railway embankment – A Vickers gun was however placed by Lt. Ryalls and a second took up position in a shell hole NE of Trones Wood, the Coy in Waterlot Farm at the same time opened rapid fire on the advancing enemy. Though the enemy made repeated attempts to work round the S end of Waterlot Farm the cross fire of these two guns and the rifle fire always checked any advance. Enemies casualties up to this point were at least forty – A platoon was sent up to reinforce the Garrison of Waterlot Fm. Artillery had been meanwhile asked for and was obtained at 4.30pm. The enemy retired leaving however some snipers in shell holes who caused considerable loss until dominated by the snipers of the garrison.

On the NE of the farm, meanwhile, a Coy of the enemy emerged from Delville Wood and got into the German trench, moving along it in the direction of Guillemont. At the same time the enemy, strength one battalion, moved out of this trench in six lines and advanced on the farm – 2nd Lt Scofield who was at the time in command of the platoon on the NE of the farm, opened with his Lewis gun and rapid fire at 300 yds range. The enemy who was in very close formation did not stand this fire for long, an officer was seen trying to rally his men, but they eventually retired into the trench from which they had advanced – During this attack 2nd Lt Scofield was dangerously wounded, and has since died, - Sergt Cook who took over command of these two platoons estimated the enemy's casualties during the attack at 500, he states that this is if anything an underestimation – There is no doubt the enemy was surprised to find this trench held in such strength, it had been occupied unseen and every endeavour had been made to keep it as a surprise.

On the 19th no infantry attack was made by the enemy on Waterlot Fm, but the whole line held by the Battn was very heavily bombarded during the day, the bombardment was continuous and frequently intense – the trench held by Sergt Cook was obliterated and rendered untenable – What remained of this garrison with the Lewis gun was buried three times but recovered and remained in action – The evacuation of this trench exposed Lt Ryalls left flank, but this was covered as far as possible by a Vickers And Lewis gun in the strong point West of Waterlot Fm – The Farm was handed over to the 14th Glosters on the night of the 19th July. At 8.30pm on the 19th July a patrol reported the enemy advancing from Guillemont on Trones Wood – An officers patrol was sent out to confirm this, but he reported an advance on the part of the enemy

Word had meanwhile been sent to the Glosters who were on their way to take over the trenches and on the arrival of two of their Coy's in support the whole line was very strongly held – Our artillery had at this time opened a heavy fire on the enemy's trenches north of Guillemont which probably stopped any intended attack – The following casualties occurred during these operations.

Officers killed Lt A C Stiles
Wounded 2 Lt A M Mclaren (since died), 2/Lt R P Scofield (since died), 2/Lt W H Findley, Capt & Adj C Johnson, Lt Col R Browne-Clayton, Maj R Worthington, Lt H D Ryalls, 2/Lt J A Blake
Lt Col Browne- Clayton, Maj Worthington and Lt Ryalls were however slightly wounded and remained at duty.
Other Ranks – Killed Battery Sergt Maj Giles and 31 NCOs and men wounded 175, missing 7, shell shock 5, accidentally injured 1, sick 1

Fred was killed in the action at Trones Wood, on the 19 July 1916, aged 32 but was one of the missing. His body was never found but his mother kept a candle burning in the window at home in the hope that he would return. The following was reported in the local paper.

Wiltshire and Gloucestershire Standard 12th August 1916

There have been two services in St John the Baptist's Church, "In Memoriam" for Messrs Frederick George Souls and Walter Davis Souls, who have lost their lives fighting for their country. This is the third memorial service in one *family. Much sympathy is felt for the bereaved parents. The "Dead March" was played in each instance. Mr Philip Brook, churchwarden, was present. Mr F Surch took the sexton's duty in the management of the passing bell.*

Fred's name carved on the Thiepval Memorial

Fred is commemorated on the Thiepval Memorial to the missing, on the Somme and his photo can also been seen on the panel of 600 missing, in the Visitors Centre.

Walter Souls

17209 Private W D Souls Machine Gun Corps

AT THE BEGINNING of July 1916, Walter was with his machine gun unit at Camblain D'Abbe. Here they cleaned their weapons, paraded, practiced drill and were able to enjoy a bath. Walter would have been busy checking his equipment and Vickers Machine Gun. He probably had time to write home to his parents and play a few card games with his pals.

The Vickers machine gun is fired from a tripod, and is cooled by water held in a jacket against the barrel. The gun weighed about 28lbs and the water another 10 with the tripod weighing 20 pounds, 58lbs in all. Bullets were assembled into a canvas belt, which held 250 rounds and the gun could be fired at a rate of 500 rounds per minute. There were five men in a team with two carrying the gun, two the ammunition and one acting as a spare man.

War Diaries 5th Brigade Machine Gun Company

19.7.1916
Company standing by ready to move. Steady drill and inspection of rifles, iron rations etc.

20.7.1916
The Company paraded at 12.30a.m. Marched to Pernes and entrained there. Train left about 4.50a.m. Company detrained at SALEUX and marched to billets at CORBIE via AMIENS. Reached billets at 11.30p.m.

Walter was probably unaware that the day before and a few hundred yards away, his brother Fred had gone over the top with the 16th Cheshires, never to be seen again.

27.7.1916
No Infantry action took place. Casualties, 1 OR wounded. Two guns supported attack of 99th Brigade on Delville Wood, under Lt. R.G. Kinsey.

28.7.1916
Casualties, 1 OR killed, 3 OR wounded. Section relief carried out.

29.7.1916
C section moved from reserve, up to font line South of WATERLOT FARM. Casualties, 4 OR wounded. Attached men. 7 OR wounded.

On the 30 July, the 2nd Ox and Bucks Light Infantry and the 24th Fusiliers, supported by the 5th Brigade Machine Gun Company, went forward from Waterlot Farm towards Guillemont Station, but were forced to withdraw. This was the same day that Lol Lane, Oliver Porter and Will Pill were with the 8th Glosters attacking the Switch Line at High Wood.

War Diaries 5th Brigade Machine Gun Company

30.7.1916
At 4.45a.m. 2nd Oxf and Bucks L.I. attacked GUILLEMONT STATION. 2

guns of C section were taken forward under 2/Lt. T. W. Walding, but returned, owing to failure of attack. One gun was fired on the enemy's reinforcements conflicting considerable loss. Casualties, 3 OR wounded, 1 OR missing.

Walter was wounded in the left leg during this action. He would initially have been treated at a Regimental Aid Post just behind the frontline. From here he would have passed to an Advanced Dressing Station and then to a Field Ambulance.

His wound was serious so he was sent on to a Casualty Clearing Station, which was generally a large tented camp several miles behind the lines and then was transferred to the 25th Stationary Hospital in Rouen, for treatment. It was here that Walter died, aged 24, from a blood clot following an operation on 2 August 1916 and he is buried in St Sever cemetery.

Walter's grave in St Sever cemetery, Rouen

His mother received a letter from M. Phillips, Matron at the hospital.

> 'Dear Mrs Souls, I much regret to have to tell you that your son died very suddenly about nine o'clock yesterday evening.

He came to us with a wound in his left leg, and on Tuesday he had to undergo an operation, but he rallied and seemed to be better. He was quite cheery, and then the next evening he suddenly collapsed and died instantly from an embolism (or clot of blood) in the heart. I am enclosing a postcard, which he wrote on the day he died. He will be buried in the little British cemetery just outside Rouen where lie other brave lads who have fallen in this dreadful war. This will be a dreadful blow to you and you have our deepest sympathy in your great loss.'

The hospital chaplain also wrote the following words to Mrs Souls.

'Dear Mrs Souls - I presume you have already received the news of the death of your son. It came rather unexpectedly and suddenly. It was only the day before that I had seen him. He seemed quite happy, and little did I think that he was so near to the end, but you must look upon it rather as the beginning of a new and happier life. You and he have both made a great sacrifice - you have given your son, he his life. That is what God Himself did. I pray that He may give you much comfort in your bereavement and with assurances of my deep sympathy.'

Three of the Souls boys now lay dead or missing in France. Only Alf and Arthur were left. It is not known whether they knew about their brothers, but their mother had probably written and told them.

Alf Souls

21525 Private A E Souls Cheshire Regiment

ALF AND ARTHUR were identical twins, born only an hour apart. Alf joined the 16th Cheshires, enlisting at Stow on the Wold, with Fred and Arthur but was later transferred to the 11th Cheshires who fought on the Somme and had been reduced to 100 men. Alf was in the machine gun section of the battalion, possibly a Lewis gunner.

The battalion suffered further casualties at Messines Ridge and Ypres in 1917 and fought in the rearguard action at Ploegsteert Wood in Flanders during the German Spring offensive. Ploegsteert Wood (known to British troops as Plug Street) was heavily fortified in April 1918 in an attempt to halt the German advance, but it was overrun nonetheless.

War Diaries 11th Battalion Cheshire Regiment

8.4.1918
On the night of the 8th the Bn relieved the 2nd South Lancs Regt. The Bn. held the line on the south side of PLOEGSTEERT WOOD.

10.4.1918
The enemy bombarded the front and support lines and all the back area, which increased with intensity up to 5.30aM when news came that the enemy was in LE TOUQUET STATION.

At about 5.50a.m the enemy was seen attacking up our flank coming up from the south. At the same time, parties of the enemy were seen in the rear of Battalion Headquarters which caused HQ to withdraw, and they went out in direction of PLOEGSTEERT WOOD, being fired at the whole time from the direction of Lancashire Support Farm, and on passing PLOEGSTEERT VILLAGE, parties of enemy opened machine guns.

Lieut Col G Darwell MC was hit whilst withdrawing his Headquarters and the command passed to Maj E Prior DSO MC who had gone to Brigade to give them the situation. Orders were then issued for us to form a line in rear of the 23rd South Lancs Bn astride the PLOEGSTEERT-ROMARIN ROAD, (sheet 28T.29.2.9.7). This line was held until midday the 11th. The Bn then took up a position on the right of the South Lancs Regt. Facing south, and at 12 midday the whole line was attacked and driven back to the Army Line. We held the line on the east side of the ROMARIN-NEUVE EGLISE RAD. Orders came that the right flank of the Bn on our right was in a dangerous position, so we were called out to form a defensive flank along the KOEPEPYP Road, but shortly after the situation cleared up and we took up our position again in the Army Line.

At 7p.m. the Bn moved to PONT D'ACHELLES to dig a line from ROMARIN to PONT D'ACHELLES. This line was started on but finding the enemy were in occupation of ROMARIN, a line was dug about 200yds in rear of the ROMARIN- PONT D'ACHELLES and occupied until 4p.m. 12th, with the 9th Cheshires on our right, 6th South Wales Borderers on our left and the 8th Borders in support.

12.4.1918
The enemy attacked this position at 4pm and we were forced to withdraw to the KOEPEPYP ROAD, where we dug in for the night.

At 5am on the 13th the enemy attacked again and we had to withdraw to the line at RAVELSBURG, which we held until relieved.

18.4.1918
The composite Bn came out of line and we went back to the camp on the MONT-DESCATS-GODERSVE
Strength at beginning of month: 25 Officers, 853 Other Ranks
Strength at end of month: 24 Officers, 597 OR
Drafts during month: 15 Officers, 492 OR
Casualties during month: 18 Officers, 662 OR

The 11th Cheshires fell back 38 miles over one 48-hour period, stopping six times to dig in. They were reduced to a handful of officers and a few exhausted survivors. It was during rearguard action at Ploegsteert Wood, Flanders, that Alf was killed on 20 April 1918, aged 31. He is buried in Strand Cemetery, Belgium, at edge of a wood.

Alf's grave at Strand cemetery, Belgium

Arthur Souls

21683 Lance Corporal A W Souls MM Cheshires

ARTHUR ENLISTED INTO the 16th Cheshires at Stow on the Wold. By 1918 he was a Lance Corporal and attached to the 7th Royal West Kents fighting in action to hold the Villers-Bretonneux Plateau 'at all costs'. This was the start of the second battle of Villers-Bretonneux and the first tank against battle of the war.

On 24 April 1918 the Germans attacked the Villers-Bretonneux Plateau using their tanks together with massive bombardment of high explosives and mustard gas to capture British forward positions. Arthur with the 7th West Kent's was called up from reserve lines and went to the assistance of the 54th Infantry Brigade. The village of Hangard was the scene of very fierce fighting especially around Hangard Wood.

Battalion War Diaries 16th Battalion Cheshire Regiment

OPERATIONS - April 24th to 27th 1918

At 7.30p.m April 24th, 7th Bn. R. W. Kent Regt. was placed under orders, GOC 54th Infantry Brigade, to take part in counter-attack in place of 11th Bn Royal Fusiliers and Battalion was concentrated in position by 8.00pm

OPERATIONS - April 24th to 27th 1918
At 7.30p.m April 24th, 7th Bn. R. W. Kent Regt. was placed under orders, GOC 54th Infantry Brigade, to take part in counter-attack in place of 11th Bn Royal Fusiliers and Battalion was concentrated in position by 8.00pm

Plan of attack
9th London Regt on right flank
7th Bedford Regt on left flank
6th Northants Regt in reserve
Attack was to pass through 58th Div. and carry their troops forward.

Artillery - A standing barrage to rest central till Z + 30 and lift to final objective till Z + 60. Protective barrage to lift 300+ east of final objective and stand for 1/2 hour.

Dispositions

A & B Coys, first wave
C & D Coys, second wave
Battn HQ's established

Narrative
At 8.30p.m. Battalion moved by companies from central by Gentelles-Cachy Road to Cachy-Domart Road. At 10p.m, A & B Coys were in position to east of road, but C & D Coys were not in position till 10.10 & 10.15p.m respectively. On the left, touch had not been established with 7th Bedfords but this was gained by B Coy during their advance. On the right, time did not allow of getting in touch with left flank of 9th Londons. As it was uncertain whether 9th Londons were in position, D Coy was held in reserve on its' arrival, to cope

with possible counter-attack from Bois Hangard, and one Coy of 6th Northants placed at disposal by OC 6th Northants was used for 2nd wave.

At 10.50p.m A & B Coys advanced. A & B Coys and part of C Coy reached final objectives and line approximate to it, but owing to heavy losses, mostly from machine-gun fire, were unable to retain and fell back. D Coy reinforced by B Coy had heaviest casualties and this caused a gap between the Battalion and the 7th Bedfords during withdrawal from objectives.

Communication was opened with 9th Londons along Cachy-Domart Road and their advance into Hangard Wood was reported to progress, but Right Flank 7th Royal West Kents Regt was unable to join up with them, though patrol during the night got in touch. During early morning, April 25th, enemy pushed patrol forward in gap under cover of mist and established MG post which impeded patrols attempting to get in touch with Right Flank 7th Bedford Regt. Enemy were consolidating in line central during morning and considerable movement was seen. At 3p.m. artillery fire was opened on them and good results appeared to be obtained.

At 4.15p.m enemy appeared to be organising attack and put on intense bombardment for one hour. Protective barrage was opened. A few of the enemy reached a point near our frontline, but the attack was not pressed. At 1.00 a.m. 26th April, the Battalion was relieved by a Moroccan Division.

Strength of Battalion going into action.
17 Officers
481 Other Ranks
Casualties
Officers: 4 wounded, 2 wounded and missing
Other Ranks: 14 killed, 85 wounded, 1 wounded and missing, 128 missing

Arthur was killed in this action 25 April 1918, aged 31, and just 5 days after his twin brother. He was awarded his Military Medal for bravery during this action.

The Royal West Kents diary for April has a Roll of Honour and Arthur is mentioned:

MM 21683 L/Cpl Souls A.W. (since a casualty) 7th Bn. Royal West Kent Regt., 53rd Infantry Brigade.

Hangard Cemetery

After the war, it is said that Annie Souls never stood for the National Anthem again. She left the village soon after to live the rest of her life at Great Barrington after unpleasant gossip about how well off she must be with the pensions from her five dead sons. Annie Souls got a shilling a week for each dead son and a letter from Prime Minister Herbert Asquith in 1916 conveying the *"sympathy of the King and Queen for Mrs Souls in her great sorrow"* after three of the boys had been killed. There was a further tragedy in the family when the youngest son Percy died from meningitis.

Arthur's gravestone

The Souls family gave the greatest sacrifice of all families in Great Rissington, with five sons killed during the Great War. Their names are read out every Remembrance Sunday in St John the Baptist Church, where the congregation face towards the war memorial. Five brothers who have tragically earned their place in history.

Tom Spencer

202023 Pte T Spencer
2/4th Gloucestershire Regiment

TOM SPENCER WAS born in Sevenhampton in 1884. He was the son of Edwin and Emily Spencer and the family moved to Great Rissington about 1885. By 1901, Tom's mother was a widow and Tom and his brothers, William and Edwin were providing for the family. Tom worked as a cowman at Rissington Hill Farm.

Tom joined the 2/4th (City of Bristol) Battalion Gloucestershire Regiment in June 1915. He was living under canvass in Epping Forest and spent the first few months getting kitted out and training for trench warfare. On 6 August 1915, the battalion was inspected by Field Marshall Earl Kitchener at Highland Park. Tom spent several months digging trenches and learning how to use a rifle. The 6th Glosters were camped nearby and on 11 September 1915 an enemy aircraft flew over and dropped bombs and incendiary devices on the two camps but no damage was done.

Tom moved to Southampton by train the following May and embarked on the SS Marguerite landing in Le Havre on 25 May 1916. Within weeks Tom was fighting in the Battle of Fromelles, which was intended to divert attention away from the Battle of the Somme in a combined action between British and Australian troops. It was a complete disaster with 1,500 British and 5,500 Australian soldiers killed, wounded or taken prisoner.

War Diaries 2/4th Battalion Gloucestershire Regiment

19.7.1916
FAUQUISSART SUB-SECN
11am Bombardment of enemy trenches commenced.
6pm Assault launched

A German counter-bombardment inflicted heavy losses before the attack began and machine gun fire from the Germans drove many of the men back to their lines. The attack was a total failure with many men killed or wounded. Of the thirty trained Lewis gunners only 20 survived. Total casualties for the battalion were seven officers and 155 other ranks.

Tom survived but was to lose his life during the Battle of Cambrai in November 1917. The attack began on 20 November using tanks to break through the German wire. The initial attack was very successful, but during a period of rest and reorganisation, the enemy prepared a counter attack. Over five days of fierce fighting most of the ground gained was lost to the enemy.

War Diaries 2/4th Battalion Gloucestershire Regiment

30.11.1917
Marched to Dainville, leaving Arras 6.50am. Entrained to BAPAUME Original intention being to march from there to BARASTRE. At BAPAUME the orders were changed and the Division transferred to 2nd Corps as enemy had broken through near GOUZEAUCOURT. Division was hurried up the line immediately on buses to RUYAULCOURT. From there Battn. marched to TRESCAULT and encamped on the S.E. corner of HAVRINCOURT WOOD arriving 6.0pm. Guards counter attacked during morning and at night and regained part of the ground.

1.12.1917
HAVRINCOURT WOOD
Battn accommodated in tents. Brigade under orders of G.O.C., 20th Division. Officers reconnoitred forward area in the morning. Orders received at 2pm for Battn. to move off at 4.30pm into line. Relieved details of 9th Sussex and

11th K.R.R. in frontline 16d and 22a (referred Gonnelieu map) 6 Glosters on left 7 Worcesters on right. Guards Division on right of 7 Worcs. Battn H.Q. established in LA VACQUERIE. The relief was successfully accomplished under great difficulties as the line was held by sections of cut up units and had only been retaken on the previous day. Heavy shelling during relief: the M.O. (Capt. Robson) was killed and the RSM and 8 OR wounded (all Battn H.Q. personnel). There was no wire in front of the line taken over & there was a shortage of bombs and 2 C.T.'s led from the German line into ours. LA VACQUERIE. was heavily shelled during the night.

2.12.1917
Heavy and continuous shelling of LA VACQUERIE.. Bombing fights took place intermittently at junctions of C.T.'s joining frontline with the enemy (HINDENBURG) line. 2 prisoners were taken by right Coy in the sunken road in 21b. At 2.30pm enemy put down a heavy barrage and attacked 6th Glosters on the left causing withdrawal of part of this line and leaving a gap of about 300x with the enemy in the same trench as ourselves. 5th Warwicks came up and attacked this part at night but failed owing to thick wire. They were bombing fights all night with enemy and our left Coy joined in the frontline and in C.T.'s joining enemy frontline with ours.. There was heavy shelling of back areas during the night.

3.12.1917
Enemy attack at LA VACQUERIE. – fine frosty day

Tom was killed in action on 3 December 1917 aged 32. His body was never found along with 121 other missing men. He is commemorated on the Cambrai Memorial, Louveral. The memorial commemorates more than 7,000 men who died in the Battle of Cambrai in November and December 1917 and whose graves are not known. Tom's family also had a headstone placed in the village churchyard which simply states.

> *To the Loving Memory of Pte Thomas Spencer who gave his life for his country.*
>
> *'Nothing in my hand I bring. Simply to the cross I cling.'*

The Cambrai Memorial, Somme, France

Tom's headstone in Great Rissington churchyard

The Vellender Boys

FREDERICK AND JOHN were the sons of George and Ellen Vellender, and were both born in Cold Aston, later moving to Great Rissington in 1905. Fred was born in 1895 and John, known to his family as Jack, in 1897. Fred had bright red hair in contrast to Jack who followed the Vellender family and was raven haired. They also had three sisters, Ellen, Beatrice and Winnifred.

Jack and Fred pose in their uniforms

Fred Vellender

13812 Private F Vellender Hampshire Regiment

FRED WAS ALREADY engaged to be married when he enlisted into the army. He joined the 12th Battalion, Hampshire Regiment and served in Salonika, alongside Arthur Cyphus and Frank Mills. The 12th Hampshires were in the 26th Division, which was the last Division to be formed for the Third New Army (K3). The three men had all joined up at about the same time in 1915 and by November that year were in Salonika.

Fred left behind his fiancée, Laura Davis of Greenhills who he was sadly destined not to marry. Laura is on the left of the photo with Fred and Jack's sister Beattie standing. Although the Salonika front seemed relatively quiet, patrols and working parties could still be easy targets for the enemy. Apart from training and air raids, there was little to break the monotony of existence in Salonika. Although the climate in Salonika was very hot in summer, it was extremely severe in winter, with icy snows and winds.

War Diaries 12th Battalion Hampshire Regiment

SWITCH HILL CAMP
1.4.1917
Training of Grenadiers & Lewis gunners. All available men digging for RE's. Patrol left at 2000 & 2200. Warm

2.4.1917
Training of Grenadiers and Lewis Gunners. All available men working for RE. Patrols of 2 Officers and 2 OR left at 2000 & 2200 hrs. Warm

4.4.1917
Training of Grenadiers and Lewis Gunners. 60 men working on roads and mining for RE. At night we exchanged camps with the 10th Devons. All Coys reported present at 21.30 hrs. Lt Hale rejoined from hospital. Warm

By the 19 April Fred was at 79th Brigade Training Camp, arriving at 00.30am on the 20 April. Here the battalion took part in physical training and battle tactics.

23.4.17
Training. Striking tents and cleaning camp. At night Bn moved to
HAMPSHIRE RIDGE & DEEP CUT RAVINE CAMPS. Cold.

The 12th Hampshires moved forward in preparation for an attack. The British artillery had begun on 21 April, pouring down shells in a bombardment of the enemy's wire and trenches. The attack was to be a preliminary one to a general Allied offensive astride the River Vardar. Fred would be part of a direct frontal attack across the Jumeaux Ravine and it was timed for 9.45 p.m. The British heavy artillery continued firing without pause through the evening and throughout the first hours of darkness. At Zero hour, the whistles blew and Fred scrambled forward down the slope. The enemy fired trench mortars as the men advanced causing heavy casualties. When the 12th Hampshires reached the gaps in the enemy wire they were hit by heavy machine gun fire and were forced to lie down in shell holes for cover. The battalion had to withdraw under heavy fire back to their lines.

24.4.17
DEEP CUT RAVINE
Battalion moved from camps at 1600 hrs and marched through CT to forming up positions at MINDEN and SILBURY SUPPORT CAMP. At 2015 battalion moved by companys to position of assembly in Y RAVINE, JUMEAUX RAVINE, B10 & SUNKEN ROAD. At 2115 enemy barraged all along JUMEAUX RAVINE causing congestion and preventing companies from reaching positions of assembly before our barrage lifted at 2145. Capt Prior and 30 of A coy reported at hqrs at about 2230 as they were unable to reach their position of assembly. C Coy were then deployed in the open in front of our wire and attacked O3 & in some places gained a footing in O3 only to be driven out again by enemy barrage and enfilade fire from O2 & O4. In the operation the CO was wounded and Capt Prior assumed command. At about 2400 hrs OC DCLI took over command. Total Casualties Officers 15 OR 249.

Fred was reported missing believed killed on 24th April 1917. It is probable that he lost his life during this attack but Arthur Cyphus who served in the same battalion always maintained that Fred had been killed during a night patrol. Night patrols of two Officers and two men were still active prior to the battle and Fred could easily have gone missing at this time.

Fred was just 23 years old. He has no known grave and is commemorated on the Doiran Memorial in Greece.

The inscription on the memorial reads:

> "In Glorious memory of 418 Officers and 10,282 other ranks of the British Salonika Force who died in Macedonia and Serbia 1915–1918 and to commemorate 1979 of all ranks who have no known grave but whose names are on the panels. They did their duty.

Jack Vellender

23677 Pte J Vellender Gloucestershire Regiment

WHEN FRED CAME home on leave it inspired Jack to join up. He had admired Fred's smart uniform and, although underage, wanted to serve his country like his older brother. It must have seemed exiting adventure to the younger boy who had probably not ventured far from the village. Jack enlisted at Stow on the Wold and joined a local battalion to serve with, the 8th Glosters. He was underage and lied to the Recruiting Sergeant who conveniently turned a blind eye. Most under-age soldiers added a few years to their age to be able to join up. An estimated 250,000 British boy soldiers enlisted in between 1914 and 1915 and an estimated 120,000 were killed. Jack was to take part in the Battle of the Somme, and the war diaries record the action he was involved with at this time.

'TIL THE BOYS COME HOME

War Diaries 8th Battalion Gloucestershire Regiment

1.7.1916
Millencourt
7.30am Moved forward to Intermediate line N. of Albert
5.00pm Moved forward to valley near Albert-Pozieres road
10pm Moved forward to the Tara-Usna line in rear trenches & remained there the night.

2.7.1916
Tara-Usna Line
Battn in trenches all day

In the early hours of 3rd July the 8th Glosters were brought forward to attack the village of La Boisselle. This involved close-quarter fighting to clear the village which was slow and dangerous work.

War Diaries 8th Battalion Gloucestershire Regiment

3.7.1916
Somme, La Boisselle
57 Bde attacked and captured the village of LA BOISSELLE and also the German trenches. 400 Yards beyond, taking 153 prisoners. Following a severe bombardment and counter attack by the enemy from the direction of POZIERES, they gained the east end of the village when they were reinforced by the 10th Royal Warks and 8th Gloucs. In the end, the Germans held the line running through the church, representing a British gain of 100yds.
1.30am Moved forward to attack via ST ANDREWS TRENCH. 3.15am Attacked LA BOISSELLE & consolidated position – remained there all day and all night.

La Boiselle was eventually taken and the British sent up flares to signal the news. This provoked the Germans to launch a strong counter attack and they re-entered the village forcing the British back. The 8th Glosters commanding officer, Lt. Col. Carton de Wiart was in charge of the defence of La Boisselle and led his men in person. Jack was seriously wounded by a bayonet to his stomach

THE VELLENDER BOYS

during this hand to hand fighting and was taken to the Main Dressing Station at Albert where he died of his wounds on the 3 July 1916, the day before his 20th birthday. He is buried in Albert Communal Cemetery Extension, on the Somme. This cemetery was used by fighting units and Field Ambulances from August 1915 to November 1916. The Reverend Burgis, Senior Chaplain, wrote his mother the following letter.

"Dear Mrs Vellender,
I am so sorry that I have to write and tell you that your boy Jack died in the hospital last night, in the early hours of Tuesday morning July 3rd. He was brought into hospital a few hours before he died, wounded in the stomach, and it was fairly certain as soon as he was brought in that he would not live. I did not know your son before last night, but I am one of the chaplains stationed at the hospital, and the doctor after dressing your son's wounds, asked me to go and see him. The boy knew that he was very ill and might not recover, but he died quietly, and I do not think he was in much pain. We talked for a few minutes about life here and beyond the grave, and he told me he was ready for either. I spoke to him about his home, and he asked me to tell you that you are not to worry about his wounds and try not to be unhappy about whatever happened to him. I told him whether he lived or died he would be with God, and he answered that he believed it was so. And so the brave lad died. I am so very sorry for you, but your boy took part in a great fight for freedom and laid down his life in a noble cause. He was buried today, (Tuesday), by another chaplain as I left the hospital this morning for duty elsewhere, and his body rests in a beautiful little cemetery with some of his comrades, behind the firing line. A cross will be put up later to mark the spot. I believe Jack told me that he had a brother named Fred fighting in Salonika and I hope that son will be spared to come back at no very distant day.
Believe me
Yours sincerely
(Rev) N G Burgis CE"

A memorial service was held in St John the Baptist Church at Great Rissington, conducted by Rev Hensley on 14 July 1916. (Rev. Hensley was to lose his only son Wilfrid two years later.) The following report appeared in the *Cheltenham Chronicle*.

> *"In memory of John, son of Mr and Mrs George Vellender, who lost his life while fighting in France. The young man belonged to the 8th Gloucester Regiment, and passed away the day before his birthday, when he would have reached the age of twenty. The service was most solemn and impressive and fully attended by the parishioners in sympathy with the bereaved parents. The Rev H G Hensley conducted, assisted by Mr W Smith and choristers. The 'Dead March' was played while the congregation stood, touched with emotion."*

Jack's Grave in Albert Communal Cemetery Extension, Somme, France

Charlie White

161818 Sgt C White Gloucestershire Railway Labour Battalion (Royal Engineers)

CHARLES WHITE WAS born in 1868 in Whitnash, Warwickshire, the third son of John and Charlotte White. Charlie had lost his Mother at birth and was brought up by a farmer and his wife. His father was a Railway Plate Layer and Charlie later moved to Birmingham to work on the railways as an engineer.

Charlie married Edith Porter, sister of Oliver, from Great Rissington in 1899. They lived in Handsworth, Staffordshire in 1901, and when two children died in infancy, Edith's doctor suggested living in the country would be better for her, so they moved to Great Rissington to restart their lives.

As Charlie had been brought up on a farm and experienced with the work, he took a position at Manor Farm working for Thomas Mace. Edith and Charlie subsequently had four children Lilias 'Dolly' 1903, John 'Jack' 1905, Florence 1911 and Oliver 1917 probably named after his Uncle who died on the Somme in 1916.

At 47, Charlie was too old to join up but he was a fit man and keen to do his bit. There were announcements in the local papers for men between the ages of 41 and 47 with previous labouring and/or railway experience to join the Gloucestershire Railway Labour Battalion (Royal Engineers). Charlie went along to enlist but knocked a year off his true age, just to make sure he was accepted.

A CHANCE FOR MEN OVER THE PRESENT MILITARY AGE OF 41 YEARS.

ROYAL ENGINEERS

(REGULAR ARMY).

GLOUCESTERSHIRE RAILWAY LABOUR BATTALION.

1,000 MEN

(DIVIDED INTO 4 COMPANIES).

ONLY 500 MORE WANTED. JOIN UP AT ONCE, OR YOU WILL BE TOO LATE.

AGE - - - 41 to 47.

PAY - - - 3s. a Day.

(7 DAYS TO THE WEEK).

AND the Usual Separation and Dependants' Allowances added.

The Special Recruiting Officer will attend the following places in the TRAVELLING RECRUITING OFFICE which will be found standing in the Principal Street, and can be interviewed by men thinking of joining. At this Office any further information can be obtained; also from any Recruiting Office in Gloucestershire, Warwickshire, Worcestershire, Oxfordshire, and Buckinghamshire.

WINCHCOMBE, 9 to 9	MONDAY, May 1st.
BECKFORD, 12 to 2	TUESDAY, May 2nd.
TEWKESBURY, 9 to 9	
BROADWAY, 12 to 2	WEDNESDAY, May 3rd.
CHIPPING CAMPDEN, 9 to 2	
MORETON-IN-MARSH, 12 to 2	THURSDAY, May 4th.
STOW-ON-THE-WOLD, 9 to 9	
BOURTON-ON-WATER, 12 to 2	FRIDAY, May 5th.
NORTHLEACH, 9 to 9	" "

141

This cutting from the Cheltenham Chronicle shows where the travelling recruiting office could be found during the month of May. The 30th Railway Labour Battalion was the first unit of men of this kind to be raised in England and was chosen by the War Office because the 113th Company of Royal Engineers, also raised in

Gloucestershire, had a good reputation in Flanders for *"hard work and steadiness under any conditions."* Their pay was 3s a day with an addition of a separation allowance for dependants.

The war needed engineers to maintain railways, roads, water supply, bridges, transport, telephones and wireless. They also designed frontline fortifications and maintained guns and weapons. The 30th Railway Labour Battalion RE was formed to assist The Royal Engineers Railway Troops. Men were needed who were accustomed to hard physical labour and who were familiar with railway construction.

Charlie probably enlisted at Bourton or Stow between the 10 and 12 April 1916.

Charlie middle front wearing his Lance Corporal stripes.

He did his training at Longmoor, Hampshire where the camp had been used to train troops since the Boer War. As the French used narrow gauge tracks, these had been installed at Longmoor for training purposes before men were posted overseas. There were four companies in the battalion and Charlie is likely to have been in 'A' Company, which was the first to be posted overseas on the 17/18 May 1916. Charlie was employed in laying railway lines to the front to improve the flow of men and materials. There are no war diaries available for this battalion at the present time.

Charlie with his platoon, somewhere in France

When Charlie was demobbed he returned to Great Rissington and his old job on Manor Farm. When Major Marling bought the farm in the 1920's, Charlie worked as a Gamekeeper for the estate.

He later moved to live with his daughter, Fanny and died in 1958 a few months short of his 90th birthday. Charlie can be seen in the demob photo in the middle row third from the right.

Part Three
The Battlefields Today

VISITING THE FIRST World War battlefields of France and Belgium today is a moving experience. In the fields that were once no man's land, pieces of shrapnel, barbed wire and old munitions are still lying on the ground. During the ploughing season, farmers continue to unearth unexploded shells, known as

Hand Grenade lying on the Somme 2008

the 'Iron Harvest'. These are gathered in piles at the side of the road to await collection by the authorities.

There are also the numerous cemeteries, with their neat rows of headstones bearing the name rank and number of the soldier, where known, and the Regimental Badge of his unit. Some also have a personal message from their loved ones and these can be very poignant. About half the stones are of unknown soldiers. These bear the inscription, *'A soldier of the Great War – Known unto God'*, which was written by Kipling, whose son John was one of the missing.

Places such as Delville Wood and High Wood on the Somme and Ploegsteert near Ypres remain the final resting place for many soldiers. Woods have been replanted and have regrown with many of the missing still buried where they fell during the heat of battle. Walking in these areas is very emotive. All is so utterly quiet and peaceful; you can almost feel the silence. It is a place to reflect on the massive loss of young men's lives for a few feet of ground.

The author's son and a friend walking in Delville Wood

Newfoundland Memorial Park, Somme

The Newfoundland Memorial Park is a site that has been relatively untouched since the end of the war. It was purchased by Newfoundland in 1921 and is now owned by the Canadian Government who maintains the whole site as a memorial. It is named after the Royal Newfoundland Regiment, which provided one battalion of 800 men and is a memorial to all Newfoundlanders who fought in World War One. The park contains memorials and cemeteries to other regiments as well as preserved trench lines.

At 7:30am, on 1 July 1916, the 87th Brigade started their attack in the battle of the Somme. At 8:45am, the Newfoundlanders with an Essex Battalion were ordered to provide them with support. As the Newfoundlanders crossed the British frontline trenches they had to bunch up to pass through the gaps cut in the wire. Here they were cut down in great heaps and those behind had to climb over the dead and wounded bodies of the fallen. The forward trenches were so full of dead and dying men that the Newfoundlanders had to climb out of the trenches and advance over open ground. Out of 801 soldiers who advanced, only 69 remained standing after 30 minutes.

The author standing near the support trenches in Newfoundland Memorial Park

Thiepval Memorial

After the war, Thiepval was the site chosen for the Memorial to the Missing of those who died on the Somme and have no known grave. This huge and imposing monument was designed by Sir Edwin Lutyens and unveiled in 1932 . There are over 72,000 names of British and South African soldiers inscribed on the Portland stone panels that surround the base who died on the Somme up until 20 March 1918. The memorial also commemorates the Anglo-French Somme offensive of 1916. In recognition of this, an Anglo-French cemetery lies at the front of the memorial with 300 each of French and British burials. The following words are inscribed near the top of the memorial:

>AUX ARMEES FRANÇAISES ET
>BRITANNIQUES L'EMPIRE
>BRITANNIQUE RECONNAISSANT

'TIL THE BOYS COME HOME

Near the memorial is a visitor's centre with displays and a short film about the Battle of the Somme. There are also computers where visitors can look up names on the Commonwealth War Graves Commission database and 'Soldiers Died in the Great War'. Inside the entrance is a panel of 600 photographs that represents the missing men on the memorial. Among these photos are Garnet Morris, Fred Souls and Oliver Porter whose names are carved on the memorial.

The Missing of the Somme

THE BATTLEFIELDS TODAY

Thiepval Memorial

Lochnagar Crater, Somme

Lochnagar Crater was created by a huge mine exploded under the German lines on 1 July 1916. It left a hole 300 ft across and 90ft deep. The crater was purchased by Richard Dunning and preserved as a memorial. On the anniversary of the Battle of the Somme, at 7.30am, 'Friends of Lochnagar' hold a service of remembrance at

Lochnagar crater in 2004

the cross near the entrance. La Boiselle village is nearby where Jack Vellender was wounded.

Below is a photograph of one of the most touching messages I have seen, left at the Lochnagar Crater.

The Menin Gate, Ypres (Ieper)

Ypres was known as Wipers to the Tommies. The Menin Gate was the start of one of the main roads out of Ypres towards the frontline. Most men passed through it and along the Menin Road on their way to the front. George Rachael would have passed through here on his way to the trenches and it was near here that Will Bolter worked on the railway lines. The Menin Gate memorial was designed by Sir Reginald Blomfield with sculpture by Sir William Reid-Dick and was unveiled on 24 July 1927.

The gate is more of an archway with huge panels into which are carved the names of 54,896 men from Britain, Australia, Canada, India and South Africa who died in the Ypres salient prior to 16 August 1917 (with some exceptions) and have no known grave.

THE BATTLEFIELDS TODAY

The Menin Gate

Every night at 8.00pm the traffic is halted and buglers from the Ypres Fire Brigade play the 'Last Post'. The Last Post at the Menin Gate is a very moving experience as you look at the thousands of names carved in stone and listen to the sound of the bugles.

Keep the Home Fires Burning,
While your hearts are yearning.
Though your lads are far away
They dream of home.
There's a silver lining
Through the dark clouds shining,
Turn the dark cloud inside out
'Til the boys come home.

Abbreviations And Terms Used In War Diaries

2/Lt - Second Lieutenant
Adj – Adjutant
Bde - Brigade
Blighty - England, Britain, Home
Bttn, Btn, Bn – Battalion
Capt – Captain
Cas _ Casualty
CB- Confined to Barracks
CO - Commanding Officer
Col - Colonel
Coy - Company
Cpl - Corporal
CRT- Canadian Railway Troops
CT - Communication Trench
DCLI - Duke of Cornwalls Light Infantry
DLI - Durham Light Infantry
DGQ - Divisional Headquarters
GHQ- General Headquarters
HE - High Explosive
HLI- Highland Light Infantry
HDQS - Headquarters
Infty - Infantry
KOSB - Kings Own Scottish Borderers

KOYLI - Kings Own Yorkshire Light Infantry
KRR - Kings Royal Regiment
Lancs Fus - Lancashire Fusiliers
L/Cpl - Lance Corporal
Maj – Major
MG - Machine Gun
MGC - Machine Gun Corps
MO - Medical Officer
NCO - Non Commissioned Officer
OC - Officer in Charge
OR - Ordinary Rank
RDC Royal Defence Corp
Regt - Regiment
Rgt - Regiment
R. Insq - Royal Inniskilling
RSM - Regimental Sergeant Major
RWS (Queens) - Queens West Surry Regiment
Sgt - Sergeant
SLI - Somerset Light Infantry
TM - Trench Mortar

Resources

Tommy Goes To War (2004) Malcolm Brown

Kitchener's Army (2003) Ray Westlake

With a Machine Gun to Cambrai (1969) George Coppard

Tommy: The British Soldier on the Western Front (2005) Richard Holmes

Anthem for Doomed Youth (2002) Jon Stallworthy

To the Last Man: Spring 1918 (1993) Lyn MacDonald

Somme (1993) Lyn MacDonald

The Long, Long Trail
www.1914-1918.net/

The Western Front Association
www.westernfrontassociation.com/

Reveille Press
www.reveillepress.westernfrontassociation.com/

The Commonwealth War Graves Commission
www.cwgc.org/

Ancestry
www.ancestry.co.uk

The National Archives
www.nationalarchives.gov.uk/

(WO 95 war diaries)

The Soldiers of Gloucestershire Museum
www.glosters.org.uk

NOTES

Reveille Press

FOR A FREE GUIDE TO PUBLISHING
YOUR MILITARY HISTORY BOOK
visit www.reveillepress.com

Reveille Press is a dedicated
First World War publishing service
designed exclusively for
Western Front Association members.

It is brought to you by
Tommies Guides Military Book
Specialists in partnership with the WFA.

Now, for the first time, authors whose
work would not attract mainstream
publishing houses, can gain
cost-effective access to professional
publishing services marketed
at their genre.

Web: www.reveillepress.com
Email: books@reveillepress.com
Telephone: +44 (0)845 475 1945
Facsimile: +44 (0)870 622 1918

Reveille
PRESS